What Would Dolly Do?

What Would Dolly Do?

HOW TO BE A
Diamond in a Rhinestone World

A Spirited Homage to the Queen of
Country

LAUREN MARINO

GRAND CENTRAL
PUBLISHING

NEW YORK   BOSTON

Grand Central Publishing
Hachette Book Group
1290 Avenue of the Americas, New York, NY 10104
grandcentralpublishing.com
twitter.com/grandcentralpub

First Edition: April 2018

Grand Central Publishing is a division of Hachette Book Group, Inc. The Grand Central Publishing name and logo is a trademark of Hachette Book Group, Inc.

The publisher is not responsible for websites (or their content) that are not owned by the publisher.

The Hachette Speakers Bureau provides a wide range of authors for speaking events. To find out more, go to www.hachettespeakersbureau.com or call (866) 376-6591.

Illustrations by Monika Roe.

Library of Congress Control Number: 2018932564

ISBNs: 978-1-5387-1300-6 (paper over board), 978-1-5387-2199-3 (ebook)

Printed in the United States of America

LSC-C

Printing 5, 2020

Contents

Author's Note

When Andy Warhol asked Dolly Parton in *Interview* magazine if she kept a diary, she said, "I don't have to. It seems like for the last 40 years my life has been lived in the press." In 2014, that interview was updated and she added, "I can Google any date in my history and find out what I was doing." She is highly quotable and well documented.

Dolly says she doesn't give advice; she just might give you some information that can help you out. She has enough to figure out on her own and is humble enough to resist telling people what to do. I, however, have no such qualms about telling people what to do, especially when I'm using the wisdom of the great Dolly Parton as the basis for that advice. In this book I have tried to distill all the advice she *might* give based on her stories and life and the countless interviews she has given over the past fifty years. For example, she never wrote down her own rules for a happy marriage or best ways to be creative. These lists are all based on my own research and curating and culling what I can only call the Dolly Parton philosophy, as I see it.

In pulling this book together, I have also drawn on Dolly's two autobiographies; her cookbooks and songs; books by her family members; biographies; photographs; museums and artifacts; many, many television and print interviews; visits to her hometown and Dollywood; and performances from over the last several decades.

So while Dolly didn't participate in this book, I sincerely hope that should I be lucky enough to have her become aware of it she will think that I've captured her one-of-a-kind way of looking at the world accurately and appreciates how much people can learn from her.

Introduction

Find out who you are and do it on
purpose.
—Dolly Parton

As a skinny, bookish tween, I hitched a ride with neighbors from suburban Cincinnati up to the Ohio State Fair in Columbus to see Dolly Parton just before she became a mainstream star in *9 to 5*. Cincinnati was a Midwestern town, but being on the border of Kentucky, it was also a little bit country, and Kenny Rogers and Dolly Parton were my favorites. Once inside the fairgrounds, I ignored the other amusements (pig races! butter sculpture contests!) and abandoned the people who had driven me, so focused was I on camping out on the grass in front of the stage where Dolly would play. I was an excited ten-year-old whose anticipation, combined with the feeling of camaraderie among the audience, made me feel I was among friends. When she took the stage, there was something in that lilting soprano, the energy of her performance, and how the crowd reacted to her that woke up part of my soul. It committed me forever to a love of live music. One little woman on a big stage could move this entire group of people and bring them to their feet, to tears, or to hoot, to holler, and to sing along with her. It felt like magic to me. And it felt like home.

Decades later, now a jaded New Yorker, I was in the Nederlander Theater on Broadway, starting over both personally, after a drawn-out divorce, and professionally, after a successful and satisfying twenty-five-year career ended somewhat abruptly. I had to reinvent myself, and with two small children, I didn't have the luxury of taking my time to do it. I needed inspiration. A role model. I sat through Kristin Chenoweth's one-woman show and listened as she told the audience how, growing up in Arkansas as an aspiring singer and actress, she had very few role models other than Dolly Parton. As a kid, she wanted to *be* Dolly when she grew up. As Chenoweth burst into a spirited and stirring version of "Little Sparrow," I burst into tears.

Dolly's lyrics transported me back to that state fair and my spunky, free-spirited young self, determined to see my idol. While it was her incredible energy that drew me in as a girl, it was her poignant lyrics and the emotion and life experience behind them that moved me as an adult. The lyrics are simple but the nuances of pain and strength conveyed in them connected with me deeply. I was not that little sparrow, so easily broken. I would bounce back.

After that night, Dolly's songs seemed to be playing

wherever I went. I would be out and hear "Jolene" on a juke-box or being covered by a favorite band. As one who believes in the magic of coincidences, this was becoming difficult to ignore. Yes, I know this sounds crazy, but Dolly even came to me in a dream and told me to buck up and get on with my life and, this time, have the courage to do things the way *I* wanted to do them, not the way anyone else thought I should. She reminded me I was still that independent-minded girl I had once been.

You could say I became a little obsessed. I started reading everything I could about her, listening to her music, watching her old TV interviews (go watch the 1977 Barbara Walters interview on YouTube—she is fierce!). The more I read, heard, and saw, the more fascinated I became. I was inspired. Not only is there so much more to her than meets the eye, but she is also a role model for the ages—and for all ages.

I went to Pigeon Forge and Gatlinburg, where I had vacationed growing up. I don't know if it was going back to a place I knew as a child, or having such good, clean family fun with my kids after a rough couple of years, or talking with the friendly, chatty locals, or being turned upside down three times in a row at seventy miles an hour on the Tennessee Tornado roller coaster at Dollywood. Whatever it was, it restored me in some fundamental way.

I realized that if I could learn from and find such inspiration from her, then anyone who was in my shoes could, too. She speaks openly of the hard times of her childhood;

she relentlessly pursued her dreams and didn't let anyone drag her down; she created success on her own terms—as a woman in a male-dominated (are there any that aren't?) industry. She has a sense of humor and can be silly and childlike; she has good people in her life; she brings positive energy to all that she does; she has a deep spirituality and gives back. She does it all looking fabulous with a big ole smile on her face. I might never—okay, I *will* never—be as accomplished or exceptional as Dolly, but she has many qualities I can certainly aspire to emulate.

She gave me hope and reminded me what I was made of at a time when I needed it most through both her songs *and* her example. None of us get out of this life unscathed. We only get one time around, so we need to make the most of it. There's no better example on how to do this than Ms. Dolly Parton. As a result, I find it helpful when faced with a dilemma to ask the question, "What would Dolly do?" and it makes me stand a little taller.

I'm not the only one asking that question.

The University of Tennessee in Knoxville is now offering a class called "Dolly's America: From Sevierville to the World," using the life and legacy of Dolly Parton to teach students about the history and culture of Appalachia. It's an honors course that associate professor Lynn Sacco says she came up with after hearing Dolly's U of T commencement speech in 2009. Dr. Sacco told the *New York Times* that it was a really nerdy class. A nerdy honors history course. About Dolly Parton.

The head of the history department said that she "raises

so many fundamental questions worth asking in any humanities course—about how place shapes values, our ideas about success, the relationship between art and celebrity."

As Dolly tweeted upon hearing about the course: "From the girl voted in High School 'least likely to succeed' this sure is a blessing!"

We could all use a little more tolerance, encouragement, and joy right now, as well as a reminder of what it's like to pull yourself up by your bootstraps, old-school American dream–style. From a whip-smart and talented woman who does things her way. Hopefully she will inspire you and your own dreams, whatever they might be, just as she inspired me.

Dollyisms

Some call her the "Dolly Lama" or the "Dolly Mama" because of her plethora of down-home wisdom, humorous one-liners, and self-deprecating jokes. Dolly Parton is famous for her Dollyisms, from "Don't get so busy making a living that you forget to make a life" to "If you see someone without a smile, give them yours." But beneath the quips is a complex, hard-driving, intelligent, and deeply spiritual woman.

While a prolific songwriter, she is also quite creative in dealing with the press. Having done so many interviews and being asked so many of the same questions over and over (about her "invisible" husband, her bosom, her relationship with her best friend, her flamboyant appearance), she started to provide humorous answers. Answers that may or may not have been 100 percent true. As time went on, she started to provide these answers again and again, sometimes embellishing them, and the media and the public just ate it up. Having a sense of humor and being able to laugh at herself shows her self-awareness, intelligence, and wit. And these words of wisdom, tall tales, and exaggerations serve two purposes: They get a laugh and they give her an easy way to handle intrusive questions. In both of her autobiographies, she even includes a list of popular questions she gets and includes the answers she has come up with.

When Dolly puts a show together, she will sit down and write some funny things or jokes, and since she tends to think in rhyme and phrases, she can easily come up with a good one-liner. She also improvises a lot onstage, depending on the show, and when something works, she will use it again. She has been using "It costs a lot of money to look this cheap" for years and years, and it still gets a laugh. When you do the number of shows she does, or the number of interviews where the same questions get asked over and over again, it is worth having some structured answers. She is just more creative and deliberate about it than most people.

What Would Dolly Do?

Chapter One

Put Wings on Your Dreams

*D*olly Rebecca Parton was born in 1946 near the Little Pigeon River in the foothills of the Great Smoky Mountains of East Tennessee. She was the fourth child of twelve—after Willadeene, David, and Denver and before Bobby, Stella, Cassie, Randy, Larry, Floyd, Freida, and Rachel—born in a two-room wooden cabin with no toilet, shower, or electricity. When the doctor came to deliver her, he was paid with a bag of cornmeal because her parents had no money.

So began the journey of one of the world's most enduring, successful, and beloved singers, a self-described "Cinderella story, the rags-to-riches kind." Her father was a sharecropper and sometimes construction worker or coal miner, and her mother, as Dolly says, was pregnant so much she always had one baby on her and one in her. The children had many chores and minimal entertainment, other than an old battery-operated radio that, when it was working, would occasionally bring *The Lone Ranger* or the music of Hank Williams and the Carter Family singing at the Grand Ole Opry into their house.

Dolly grew up in poverty and she speaks of it openly: "We didn't have the things we wanted but we didn't starve...we were hungry for a variety of things but as far as going hungry with our bellies empty, we never had to do that. We just had simple things. Like for breakfast we always had just gravy and biscuits. For dinner and supper we had beans and potatoes. We were lucky to have it." Much of what they ate they grew or shot themselves.

Her father labored so hard his hands and feet would bleed. Her mother prepared and cooked meals, made their clothes, and did countless other chores. In her song "In the Good Old Days (When Times Were Bad)," she writes about getting up before the sun to work in the fields only to watch a hailstorm destroy those crops, or waking up with ice and snow on the floor and watching her parents suffer through overwork and illness. She says that there is no amount of money that would be enough to make her go back and live through those times again.

Given her parents' never-ending responsibilities, little Dolly was alone a lot. They had no TV or movies and very limited reading material, so she learned to entertain herself. She would find quiet spaces to sit and just stare at the clouds for hours at a time, dreaming and making up stories, playing out fantasies in her mind. The perfect escape for a child who didn't like school and did whatever she could to get out of working in the fields was "fairy stories, fairy tales. I used to just live in them." They used old newspapers as wallpaper in their two-room cabin and so she would read the walls. Her imagination was so active that she would create lives and stories around the people and things she read about.

Soon she moved on to creating fairy tales with herself at the center of them. She began imagining and planning a better life for herself. She loved writing songs and performing from a young age and realized that her talent and passion could help her achieve the big life she wanted. The difference between Dolly and the majority of people is that she not only believed deep down in her soul that her vision would come true, but she also did everything in her power to make it happen. She says, "I'm a dreamer, but I'm a doer, too." She took those hard times and created music from them. She was a self-taught singer, musician, and songwriter with minimal education, but her ambition, drive, and relentless work ethic made her a star.

Young Dolly had plenty of time to run wild, to dream, and to gain admiration by making up little songs. Her first, "Little Tiny Tassel Top," composed at age five, was an ode to her corncob doll with corn-silk hair that her father had made for her. She had her mother write down the lyrics. She says that "when people would come around, Mama'd say, 'You gotta hear this little song Dolly wrote!' I loved it, of course, and I thought, 'Well, I'll stay with it.'" She would stand on the porch, pretending she was onstage, and sing to the chickens and younger children with a tin can on a tobacco stick as a microphone.

By the age of eight, she was performing at the Church of God, where her grandfather preached, and went around singing in other churches with her siblings as the Parton Sisters. Her entire family was musical and she claims she wasn't the most talented but she was "the one with the dreams and the confidence. From the time I was little I always loved music."

She was determined to get out and see the world beyond her own hills. "I learned there was this place you could go to become a star. It was called Nashville." She tells the story of having a semireligious experience as a young child: "I didn't hear a voice, but it was a knowing that came to me and it said, 'Run. Run until I tell you to stop.'"

She's been running toward her dreams ever since.

She taught herself to play chords by making herself a homemade instrument from old musical parts. Her mother's brother, Bill Owens, was the first person to recognize her talent and gave her a real guitar and taught her chords. He appreciated her determination to learn and her ability to go beyond just chords to coming up with little melodies. When she was just ten, he took her to Knoxville to audition for the *Cas Walker Farm and Home Hour*, an early-morning variety show, which was her initial break into show business. She was on television before her family even had one.

As a songwriter himself, Uncle Bill knew Nashville a bit, and when Dolly was old enough, they would drive there in his beat-up old car and try to get people to listen to their songs. "We used to come down in his rickety car any time we could beg, borrow, or steal enough money for gas. We'd clean up in service stations. I'd wash my hair in those old, cold sinks and put my makeup on in the mirrors in the car." She would stand outside the Country Music Hall of Fame and look at all the famous names written on the pavement and vow to herself that someday her name, too, would be there. (It is.) Through it all, she says, "There wasn't ever a time I thought I wasn't going to make it."

If anyone ever figured out the American dream and made it work, it's Dolly Parton. Her ability to imagine a better future for herself, as well as her hard work and determination, got her out of the holler. How did she achieve her dreams against all odds?

"I wake up with new dreams every day. And the more you do, when you're a dreamer, the more everything creates other arenas you can go into. It's like a tree with many branches, and branches with many leaves."

If You Don't Like the Road You're On, Start Paving a New One

Even though she had her family and their love, and despite the somewhat romanticized view of her past that she presents now, Dolly craved to see the world beyond the foothills of the Smoky Mountains: "I had my songs to sing. I had an ambition and it *burned* inside me. It was something I knew would take me out of the mountains."

What is a dreamer except a person who believes that the impossible can become possible? As children, we daydream and imagine who or what we will be when we grow up. But once we are adults, the challenges of day-to-day reality can impinge on that ability to dream, to our detriment. Especially when we're going through challenging times, it's important to be able to imagine a brighter future. Call it hope or optimism or faith, dreaming is the belief that you can make your own life better. In Dolly's own words, "You can think yourself rich or you can think yourself poor." While it's certainly more complicated than that, her point is that your thoughts and aspirations are powerful and that being able to imagine yourself being successful is the first step to getting there. Whatever success you might have, it all starts with a vision of what is possible.

She is a big believer in using and exercising her own mind's power to make things happen for herself and carves out time and space to dream. At a young age, she started paving a new road for herself, saying, "I dreamed of the time that I'd have money and I'd be rich and I would have pretty clothes and makeup and jewelry and houses and cars— big cars and houses. I just dreamed of all the things that I would have. And I dreamed of singin' and I dreamed of bein' famous and loved."

But dreaming doesn't happen if you are operating on autopilot. Sometimes you need to take a time-out just to let yourself think on what it is that you want. It may seem easier said than done, but having that solitude and relaxation where you can just let your mind go on adventures is sometimes the best way to restore yourself and come up with your best ideas. As an adult, Dolly says she does her best dreaming on the front porch, and she schedules specific time to sit there alone in contemplation. Dolly's version of dreaming is songwriting or setting goals for herself. It could start with the unimaginable or what may not seem possible. But you have to start somewhere. If you want to build a business, you have to imagine it first. If you have an idea for an invention, you have to dream it up first and then map it out. If you want to be an actress, a writer, an artist, a musician, you have to picture in your mind where you want to go with it and then learn the skills required to help you get there.

Be a Dreamer, But Be a Doer, Too

It's one thing to dream of being in a fairy tale, like so many children do, but it's another to turn your life into one. You can't just sit around wishing things would happen; you have to go out there and get stuff done. Or as Dolly says, "If you never try, you ain't never going to win." Having a strong vision puts a fire in your belly that provides conviction, which, in turn, provides motivation to do the hard work required. That will sustain you, not just on your way up, but when you are beaten down and challenged, which you most certainly will be at some point.

When journalist Chet Flippo did his first *Rolling Stone* interview with Dolly back in 1977, he mentioned that she was known for setting goals and writing them down, which, he wrote, "set her off on a 45-minute discussion on achieving and how to do it." She then said she has always created elaborate and specific lists along with detailed plans on how to get things done, and then hides them away, where no one can see them. In doing so, she takes what she imagines and makes it a little more concrete, a little bit closer to reality, planting the seeds in the back of her mind. When she goes back years later and reads through these lists, she is often amazed to see that most of what she wrote down has come true: "I think, boy, if that ain't proof that positive thinkin' is a marvelous thing."

Stating your intentions and writing down your goals and dreams makes you think them through and sends a message to the universe. Dolly's list-making methods include a combination of positive thinking and visualization. If there is something that she really wants, she will "write it down on a piece of paper and I look at the list and I concentrate real hard on it, try to visualize it happening, and I just go through all the motions as if it's already been done."

Once you've written down your own list of dreams, you need to do things that will make them happen, using whatever it is you've got. The Partons were nothing if not creative in their ability to be innovative by making the most of what they had. When Dolly used to sit on the woodpile in her potato-sack dresses pretending she was onstage in sequins and silk, she played on an old mandolin she had repurposed with piano strings. "Waste not, want not" was a motto in her household, so old newspapers became wallpaper, corn husks became dolls, old scraps of cloth and rags became clothes and blankets. They made their own toys, cut down their own Christmas trees, and decorated them their way without any real ornaments. They used their imaginations. Not just in making things but in finding ways to get around things. That kind of resourcefulness and ingenuity served her well throughout her life and career and is something we can all keep in mind as we try to find our way around obstacles.

The first time Dolly was set to appear on Cas Walker's show, she happened to be there the day of Cas's greasy pole contest. Cas would grease a fifty-foot pole and put $250 at the top of it. Whoever could climb the pole and retrieve the prize money without slipping down got to keep it. Dolly watched one person after another slip down the pole. So she got an idea. She poured water on herself to get all wet, then went outside and rolled around in the dirt and sand. When her turn came, she scooted right up the pole and got the money. People were angry that she won and thought the contest had been "fixed." Cas had watched the whole thing and said, "How could a greasy pole be fixed? This girl has taught me something today and that in itself is worth $250." Dolly took the money and bought her family their very first television set, the only one in her neck of the woods. When Dolly got a spot singing on his show every Saturday, her family could now watch her on TV.

Upon arriving in Nashville she had nowhere to live or money for food, she bartered babysitting in exchange for a place to stay and filled salt and pepper shakers at a diner in return for free food. All the while she kept writing songs, knocking on doors, learning the ins and outs of the music business, and distributing demos of her songs.

Let Your Determination Be Greater than Your Fear

Dolly has said, "I always had more guts than talent." When Dolly was ten years old, she sang a song on the radio for the first time. She said she was scared to death but she did it anyway, despite her lack of experience and not knowing how to work a microphone. The crowd roared with approval and not because she was good but "just because I had the nerve to do it." Focusing on negative thoughts or fear can keep you where you are. Or you can choose to turn things around and forge ahead. One small courageous act can provide the confidence you need to climb the next step.

After her first radio appearance Dolly's confidence grew and she went on and fulfilled her first "big" dream of singing at the Grand Ole Opry at age thirteen. From there the dreams just kept getting bigger and bigger. She has said, "I've felt like my dreams were the foundation of my drive to accomplish all the things I love."

Not everyone understands that power or has the imagination to believe in a better life or future. Throughout her life, other people underestimated her; they even laughed at her. When she graduated from high school and everyone had to stand up in front of the class and say what they planned on doing, she said, "I'm going to Nashville and I'm going to become a star." There was a pause and then the whole room started snickering and laughing. She was embarrassed but she didn't let that deter her. She was on a Greyhound bus to Nashville the next morning and she told herself she wasn't going back until she made it. She didn't let the doubters drag her down. Like Dolly has said over and over, don't limit yourself just because people won't accept the fact that you can do something else or do more. Their limited imaginations are their problem, not yours. So show them what you're made of.

Dolly's drive is pretty intense but you don't get to where she is by being wishy-washy. "I've always loved what I do, and try to just do my best work. I don't try to outdo somebody else—I try to outdo me. I try to make and break my own records. I try to do better at something than I was last year."

Once you know what it is you want, never stray from it. Like Dolly says, "You can do anything you want to as long as you keep a good attitude and keep working at it. But the second you give up you're screwed." In other words, keep your mind on your business despite the inevitable bumps on the journey. Have laserlike focus. When you really know yourself and your strengths and talents and are willing to make the necessary sacrifices to get what you want, to be who you want, well, you almost can't lose.

When she boarded that Greyhound bus, it was the first time she had ever left her family and, after saying goodbye to them, she wept for the entire ride. Once she got to Nashville, she was broke and homesick, hungry and constantly getting rejected. She wrote some pretty sad letters home and spent many a lonely night crying herself to sleep. It took some time for her to get established: "The first few months I was afraid, but my determination was greater than my fear, and my confidence was greater than my fear. I knew I would have a hard time, but when you're used to doin' without you don't get afraid of what you're gonna have to do without." She persisted and about six months after getting there she managed to get $50 a week from Monument Records writing songs. From there things started to improve, bit by bit.

There's no such thing as an overnight success. Dolly says, "I've kept on keeping on. And I never let a person, nor a thing, nor a sickness, nor a heartache, nor anything keep me from keeping on." Anyone who becomes successful has gone through the hard work, sacrifice, occasional self-doubt, and persistence required to make it.

When Dolly got her first big break in 1967 working with Porter Wagoner on his top television show, she was replacing his beloved "girl singer," Norma Jean. His audience loved Norma Jean, and when she got pregnant and left the show to get married, they resented that Dolly was there to take her place. For the first several shows, the audience would shout out, "Norma Jean, Norma Jean" every time Dolly got up to sing. She spent many nights feeling insecure before going onstage. It may have hurt her but she didn't let it break her. It took all of her guts and determination to keep going and to make them accept her. Night after night she just kept singing her heart out, smiling and building a great rapport with her boss, and eventually the audience. In retrospect, she says that trying to win over the audience became a "little inspiration" for her. She thought to herself, *I'll make them forget Norma Jean.* And, boy, did she ever.

She ended up working with Porter on the show for seven years and became a huge success, not just as a performer but also as a songwriter, her star power eventually outshining that of her boss.

Dream More

Dolly believes you can will and dream yourself to be anything you want to be, and that philosophy is the very basis and brand of her more recent endeavors. She made her own dreams come true and now she wants to inspire others to do the same. The guiding principles of her Dollywood Foundation and the Imagination Library are to help instill values in children—well, in everyone really—to "dream of doing more with your life, learn from everything you see and do, care for everyone and everything that crosses your path, and be more than you ever dreamed you could become." Her 2009 commencement speech at the University of Tennessee shared these ideals, and her most recent book, *Dream More*, takes what she said in that speech and goes even further with it by using stories from her own life to show others how to do it. She is so committed to this concept that she even named her 2015 hotel near Dollywood the DreamMore Resort.

She preaches the idea of positive thinking and never giving up like her grandfather preached fire and brimstone. She told biographer Alanna Nash in the book *Dolly*, "A lot of it comes from my religious background, but it's really just my true nature to be a positive person. I've read those books about havin' a positive attitude, but they just told me things I already believed. In fact, readin' 'em was just like I was sayin' it to myself." She believes in this concept so strongly that she wants to share it to inspire others to go after their own dreams.

Keep Dreaming New Dreams

Fulfilling your deepest aspirations has a cumulative effect. When you get over the initial learning curve and show yourself that what you envision is more than the stuff of daydreams, you can move on to the next thing and the next one after that. Once you've accomplished what you initially set out to do, it is only natural to become more confident and rise to the next challenge. Once you've fulfilled a specific goal, you can come up with new ones.

Dolly knows how fortunate she is to have seen her life's desires come true and that sense of gratitude is pervasive in all that she does. She has said that there are people who are a lot more talented than she is and who have worked just as hard but for whatever reason, they have not made it big the way she has. Was she just the right person at the right time? Was she just lucky? There are many "what ifs" to anyone's success, but the best thing you can do is constantly evaluate your progress and stay persistent and optimistic regardless of the occasional beat-down. No matter what, never give up or rest on your laurels. No matter how old you get or how accomplished, there are always new horizons to explore.

After her first appearance at the Grand Ole Opry she dreamed of going to Nashville and becoming a star, and she did it with Monument Records and *The Porter Wagoner Show*. She dreamed of going out on her own as a successful solo artist, and she did it. She then dreamed of having mainstream success and working in Hollywood, and she did it. She dreamed of going back to the Smoky Mountains and honoring her people by starting a theme park devoted to her culture, and she did it. She dreamed of writing children's books and producing family-oriented and children's TV shows and albums, and she did it. She dreamed of helping children learn to love reading and helping solve the literacy problem in the area where she grew up, and she did it. With each step she took and each mountain she climbed, she immediately dreamed a new dream and started climbing again. She never stopped; she was never stagnant. One led to the next and the next after that.

Not long before she turned seventy, she said, "This point is probably the greatest time in my entire life because I can make the choices I need to. I don't have to worry about the things you used to when you started out, like money and all of that. But I still enjoy the work. One dream leads to something else, so I am going with the flow and going where God leads me."

Iron Butterfly: Gentle But Determined

Butterflies have long been one of Dolly's favorite symbols, and she's included them on her album covers and her various businesses and branding. As a small child, Dolly spent much of her time in the woods and fields with little more than nature and her imagination. She loved things that she felt were sparkly and beautiful, like flowers, hummingbirds, and butterflies. She wanted to be like them. She looked at butterflies as "fancy dressed-up girls going to a party," and they inspired her. She envied their ability to fly. To her they represented the free spirit she wanted to be.

Dolly loves them because "butterflies are colorful and bright and gentle and have no way to harm you. They go about their business and bring others pleasure while doing it, because just seeing one flying around makes people happy. I'd like to think of myself as bringing people happiness while I do my business, which is my music." Over the course of her career, she became known as the original "Iron Butterfly": beautiful, gentle, but very determined.

You have to keep working at making your dreams come true. Dolly has worked her patootie off and continues to do so today. But it's not just about effort; it's also about always learning and growing and taking chances. If you fall flat on your face, at least you know that you tried and can use it as a learning experience. Learning is all about being willing to take risks, try new things, then rolling up your sleeves and doing the work—not just the physical work of doing but also the mental and spiritual work of being brave and learning from mistakes. Dolly's view is that when things don't work out as she planned, she thinks, "Well, maybe God's got something better for me." Not one to sit back and wait for whatever might happen next, Dolly has always moved on and made the best of things, even her childhood hardships. "I don't have any sympathy for myself," she says, "'cause it took all that to make all this."

WWDD TO MAKE HER DREAMS COME TRUE?

- Find the time and space to dream.
- Have a vision of what is possible and write it down.
- Don't be afraid to dream big.
- Let your determination be greater than your fear.
- Never take your eyes off the prize.
- Make the most of what you've got.
- Keep rising to the next challenge.

Chapter Two

Work Hard at Being Happy

*D*olly's rich spirit shines so bright that her costar in *The Best Little Whorehouse in Texas*, Burt Reynolds, described her as "human sunshine." She has even been inducted into the Happiness Hall of Fame at Stanford University. (Who knew there was such a thing?) She attributes a lot of that to always being grateful for her blessings and being brought up with small-town values where the most important things were God, family, and music.

Part of her optimism is just her nature and part of it is her perspective. She feels like she had a happy childhood and remembers the good times. She tells a story of an early Christmas at her house, when she was around eight or nine years old. It was the first year that the family had electric lights on their Christmas tree, and it was also the year that her daddy decided to buy her mama a wedding ring for the first time. They had gotten married when they were just seventeen and fifteen, respectively, and never had the money for one. This was going to be expensive, so her daddy explained to the kids what he was going to do but that it meant none of them would be receiving presents that year. They were so excited for their mama that they kept the secret from her and didn't mind. In order to make it fun and involve the children in the days before Christmas, Daddy said he was going to hide the ring and that whichever child found it first would receive the only other gift. He hid it in one of the electric lights on the tree by screwing the bulb off and putting it there and then screwing the bulb back on over it. Dolly says it was so well hidden that it gave them an entire day of fun looking for it. In the movie *A Christmas of Many Colors*, Dolly finds the ring and gets a box of chocolates as a gift, which she then shares with her siblings. When Christmas came and Mama opened her present, she was so happy that she cried and all of the children cried right along with her. Dolly says it was one of the best family Christmases ever, one she will always remember. Instead of feeling deprived, the Parton children all shared in their parents' joy.

When Dolly was in her late thirties, she had to have a partial hysterectomy. As a result, her hormones started going haywire and she had to face the fact that she and her husband were never going to have children. She didn't feel good or look good. She was working herself to the point of exhaustion. Her best friend, Judy, was off in the army and her longtime keyboardist and confidant, Gregg Perry, left the band to become a psychologist.

It was a perfect storm of events, including an "affair of the heart" (whether her own love affair or a professional betrayal, she won't say), bleeding ulcers, a death threat, and family problems, all of which resulted in her not taking care of herself. This only snowballed and made matters worse. She was forced to cancel her tour and be on bedrest for eighteen months: "I went to the bottom as far as my emotions and health are concerned. See, I was thirty-five when I first got sick. And I was getting away with murder...I wasn't taking care of myself. I was working hard, and underneath I was a pile of personal and emotional problems. All at once I fell apart...It was God's way of telling me to get myself straight."

For many long months, she didn't work. She stayed in bed and went through a deep depression. It made her understand for the first time how people can become addicted to drugs or alcohol or consider suicide. She became self-pitying, which has never been her style, and for the first time she became angry at God, demanding his help or threatening to kill herself. She says the answer came to her and she felt it was "the voice of God himself" saying, "Get off your fat butt and get on with life." For her, this moment became a turning point.

Coming out of a depressive episode isn't as easy as flipping a switch, especially if it's clinical, but for her this approach worked. She decided to get up and focus on the positive, and little by little, she recovered. Now she'll occasionally get into moods, but feels "if you never get depressed, you're never ever getting down deep enough to think about things.

Nobody's up all the time unless they're liars, phonies, hypocrites, or unless something in their brain ain't working." That said, she won't allow herself to be depressed, or wallow, for more than three days in a row. When she knows she is in a funk or a bad place, she will do what she has always done and get out a piece of paper and make one of her lists. She writes down all of the good things in her life and all that she is grateful for. Then she picks herself up, fixes herself up, talks to a friend, or focuses on doing something nice for someone else.

Her happiness is part of her natural-born disposition, but it is also something she works at. It is grounded in a strong sense of self-awareness, an independent spirit, and a rock-solid spiritual foundation.

"I was born with a happy heart. I'm always looking for things to be better."

If You Want the Rainbow, You Have to Put Up with the Rain

Dolly thinks it's better to feel your feelings and deal with them, as uncomfortable as that may be. Suppressing them is only going to make them show up when you least want them to. Dolly says that as a songwriter, "I have to not harden my heart, because I want to stay open to feel things. So when I hurt, I hurt all over. And when I cry, I cry real hard. And when I'm mad, I'm mad all over. I'm just a person; I like to experience whatever the feeling is and whatever I'm going through."

She even wrote a children's book called *I Am a Rainbow* that associates colors with different emotions to help children understand their feelings. You can be tickled pink with happiness or be green with envy or be plain blue with sadness. It's all part of being alive. Plus, having a rich range of emotions makes you a much more interesting person.

Despite her upbeat nature and phenomenal success, she is only human and it can be easy to forget that she is also a sensitive artist who has suffered her share of dips and valleys. Many of her lyrics are downright haunting in the misery they describe. "I'm *not* always happy—that would be a very shallow person," she says. Or as she says in her more playful moments, "I'm not happy all the time; that's just the Botox."

Dolly's attitude is that, in many cases, happiness is a choice and it can start in your own heart and mind. She says that some people work hard at being miserable; she works hard at being happy. She even has her own self-created self-help philosophy called IAM (individual awareness method) that she uses to help her with everything from overcoming depression, to mending a broken heart, to losing weight. Essentially she uses deep reflection, self-awareness, and thoughtfulness to become aware of why she does what she does and to figure out what she needs to do to make herself better.

Her approach made the link between her mental and physical well-being, long before the idea of the mind-body connection went mainstream. She came to realize that "a lot of my physical problems stemmed from my emotional ones. I felt the good Lord would give me strength to let my body eventually heal itself and that I'd be okay if I could get that positive attitude going, get my mind straight, draw from the energy God has given me."

In other words, feel your feelings but don't get mired in the mud. At a certain point you've got to figure out where the unhappiness is coming from and then set about fixing it. No one can avoid rough patches in life, and as unpleasant as they might be, devastating even, you can use those times for personal growth. It's important to look at the tough times in life as growing pains. They hurt when they're happening but you can come out of them stronger and better equipped to handle the next time things aren't going so well. As Dolly has said, "I'll never harden my heart, but I've toughened the muscles around it."

Dolly now looks back on those physical and mental health issues as the best things that ever happened to her. They made her realize that she could never retire because she loved her work, and that realization broadened her career and reach. She also had to reconcile with the fact that she was never going to be a mother and decided that she would view the world as her children and give them—her family, her fans, her friends, her employees—everything she had. By making the people of the world her children, she began her work as a philanthropist, giving back and changing other people's lives on a much larger scale than ever before.

We all have times when we have to put up with the rain. The way to get through it is to find your therapy. Whether it's a shrink, church, a spiritual coach, a creative outlet, journaling, yoga, meditation, or faith in a higher power, find a way to work through your moods. While Dolly's faith has always carried her through, she also says that music is her primary therapy. Her songwriting is a cleansing exercise of its own. She said early in her career that writing songs is "better than a psychiatrist because I'm able to put the hurtin' things into my songs and then they don't hurt me anymore." Her songs are so honest and so much a reflection of her life or experiences that getting her thoughts down on paper is a way for her to heal.

She says that the pain she always kept inside of her after being bullied and teased at school for wearing the patchwork coat her mother made out of rags finally disappeared after she was able to sit down and write "Coat of Many Colors." She told the story, got it out of her system, and turned it into art and something positive. Her most enduring and successful songs come from writing about life's difficult emotions. Processing your pain and feelings can be done in so many ways, so find what outlet works for you.

Dolly's Spiritual Purification Exercises

In her 1994 autobiography, *My Life and Other Unfinished Business*, Dolly shared a few of the spiritual exercises she uses to get rid of negative thoughts, stay positive, and move on with a fresh attitude. For Dolly, spirituality and self-improvement programs and practices go hand in hand with being happy. She has a specific method she outlines that may seem complicated but can be tailored to your own needs:

Affirmations: She regularly uses positive words and affirmations to make herself feel good: "I am encircled by light," "I am radiant," "Nothing can harm me," "I am happy," and other positive sayings along those lines that help her rise above whatever negativity or struggles she is dealing with on any given day.

Visualizations: She will go somewhere quiet, usually one of the chapels or meditation areas she has in each of her homes, and imagine herself surrounded by light. She pictures God turning her upside down and shaking all negativity out of her body—it falls out of her like loose change and lands in the circle of light. Then she visualizes light streaming out of her head and feels that she is becoming the light. After that, she and God grind all of the negativity that came out of her into a fine powder and she blows on it so that it disappears. Be gone, negativity!

Write it down: She takes three notebooks or notepads and devotes each one to a specific subject. In the first, she writes down all the things that are bothering her, holding her back, or generating negative thoughts, anger, or frustration. In the second notebook, she writes about all the things that she is grateful for, including all of the positive things around her and the positive qualities of the people she may be having trouble with at the moment (easier said than done!). In the third notebook, she writes down all of her hopes, dreams, wishes, and desires. You can tailor this exercise in whatever way works best for you.

From there, she holds her notebooks up to the light and asks God to cleanse her, to forgive her, and to take into account all she has written and to put the pieces of her life back together in a way that is whole. From there, she rips the pages she's written out of the notebooks and burns them—in a safe way!—watching them disappear into ashes. The smoke going up to the heavens is an offering of sorts. Then she looks at the clean, white pages that are left in the notebooks. That is her blank slate, her fresh page. From there, she can start anew.

"Being a star just means that you just find your own special place and that you shine where you are."

Shine Where You Are

One of Dolly's mottos that she has followed in pursuit of her own happiness is "To thine own self be true." Knowing who she is, where she belongs, and that she can shine are all a big part of her journey. Her mama, Avie Lee, instilled that in all of her children. Dolly was always going to follow her own heart and her own path and speak her mind. If other people didn't like it, well, she wasn't going to let it get her down. That strong sense of self and purpose was deeply intertwined with her well-being. Her mama told her, "Don't try to be what somebody else wants you to be. Listen to your heart."

One of the ways to have that type of confidence in yourself is to operate from a place of strong purpose. Ever since she was a child, Dolly knew she wanted to sing and perform; she knew she wanted to write down her thoughts and share them with the world. That drove her professionally but it also nurtured and fed her personally. Some people think that success and ambition are signs of selfishness, but for Dolly it really is about reaching as many people as she can in a positive way. She said, "I've always felt like everybody was born for a reason. Everybody has a purpose. Lots of people don't ever really find it, but I was luckier than a lot of people." It sustains her and gives her joy. We aren't all as lucky to have such a strong sense of purpose from the day we are born. Oftentimes purpose is something that comes to us over a

lifetime and it can change. Not everyone is a prodigy, but fig-
uring out what you are good at and what you are passionate
about is a good start.

It's not always easy to remain true to your sense of purpose and identity when others don't understand you. Dolly
always felt like an outsider, like she was different and wanted
to do things her own way, whether it was to dress and look
the way she wanted, develop her career the way she wanted,
or have a marriage that was the way she wanted. Being a free
spirit sometimes got her into trouble. But happiness comes
from having the courage and conviction to be yourself,
despite what others think.

Dolly says about high school: "You can be a threat to people if you have a strong identity of your own. People want you
to think just like them and be just like them and I wasn't. I
just never went by anybody else's rules. I just wouldn't con-
form." She may have suffered at times as a result, but the
pros outweighed the cons, and not dimming her light to
appease others has served her—and her happiness—over
the long run.

An example of that self-assurance was when she went
mainstream with the pop song "Here You Come Again." The
Nashville establishment was in an uproar and felt that she
had turned her back on them, but she responded by saying
she wasn't leaving country music behind; she was bringing it
with her. She also said that even though she loved her audience, she didn't fear the public. Meaning, she wasn't going
to change her music or her style because the public didn't

approve. She figured she would do what made her happy and if she wrote good music as a result, people would eventually come around to it.

Dolly's commitment to maintaining a sense of individuality shines through in her work and attitude, and as a result, Dolly's fans span demographics and the globe—hard-core country fans, drag queens, punk rockers, rappers, church-goers, rich people, poor people, gay people, straight people, city dwellers, country dwellers, North, South, black, white. She is nonjudgmental, and having felt different much of her life, she embraces and celebrates all types of people: "I never did pass judgment on anybody. I love everybody. In my early days, I was so condemned because of the way I looked or the way I acted or talked. Even now, I get a lot of that. I just look for the God-light in everybody. Everybody should shine with their own God-light."

It sort of goes without saying that if you are accepting of others and behave nicely to them, they're going to behave nicely back: "If people treat you good and love you, you love them back. That's the way I feel. I'm good to them because they're good to me. It's just a big mutual love. I want to make my fans happy because then I make myself happy." Connection is a basic human need, so the more you reach out to others, the less judgmental you are, and the more you understand that we all share common humanity, the happier you're going to be.

Dolly said in her 2009 University of Tennessee commencement speech that people remember us for who we are or were, not for how many records we sold, or dollars we made, or awards we won. She says she always counts her blessings, not her money. That a loving person is a caring person and is the best thing you can aspire to be.

Try a Little Devilment

Dolly loves to tease people and have a good time because she knows you can't always take life too seriously. She has a bawdy sense of humor and often makes herself the butt of jokes. As corny as some of her quips are, her enthusiasm in the telling always gets a laugh.

Dolly also acknowledges that she is one of God's "more mischievous angels." As a little girl, she used to take care of her grandmother Poppy, who was confined to her bed. Dolly would scrub Poppy's false teeth clean, but before returning them to her, she would put them in her own mouth, on top of her teeth, and dance around and growl like a monster.

She also likes to get into "do or dare" situations for a laugh. She was bored in school and would play little tricks or practical jokes to entertain herself, something she continues until this day. She told Chet Flippo in a *Rolling Stone* interview that she gets a real kick out of doing things that nobody would expect her to do and shared a very amusing story. She was out one night in Los Angeles with friends, including best friend, Judy Ogle, and her keyboardist and producer, Gregg Perry, during the filming of *9 to 5*. The group was driving home in two separate cars after a few margaritas at Lucy's El Adobe restaurant. Judy, who was in one car, started egging on Dolly, who was in the other car, by unbuttoning her blouse. Dolly retaliated by pulling up her shirt and flashing her. Once they started trying to one-up each other, things escalated quickly. Someone did something else and Dolly pulled down her pants and mooned them. Everyone was cracking up. Dolly knew Judy was going to try something even more risqué, so she decided to beat her to the punch and took off all her clothes at the next stoplight— right before the fancy Hotel Bel-Air. When they reached the stoplight, Dolly saw Judy open her car door and come out wearing only her pantyhose. Well Dolly just nonchalantly stepped out of her car, stark naked and snow white, and started walking around the car in the moonlight. They all almost died laughing.

Another time, on a dare, while driving through Bel Air, she took off all her clothes and streaked across sexy singer Tom Jones's front lawn. Apparently he built a fence around the property shortly thereafter!

But don't think Dolly's definition of having a good time requires running around naked. She and her husband, Carl, play a lot of jokes on each other. One time he appeared onstage, without her knowledge, dressed as one of her backup singers. Another time he taped on acrylic fingernails and walked in while Dolly was with her manicurist, asking, "Can you do anything with these nails?" He, like Dolly, is witty with a mischievous streak, which allows them to enjoy the day to day together and keep things in perspective. Being able to act silly and share laughter with someone is always going to contribute to your overall happiness.

Nurture Your Childlike Nature

Dolly says that she is still a hopeless romantic, like she was when she was a teenager. She also claims that she feels like she is thirty-five, "in my spirit and in my mind. When I was 35, it was a pinnacle, a great time in my life—success and happiness and all that. And so I just decided 'I'm gonna claim that number and always be that in my state of mind.'"

As we get older, we can lose that childlike ability to be silly or experience awe, that sense of discovery and excitement that can create so much joy. Dolly likes to think that "somewhere down inside me there's still a Garden of Eden. I'm still innocent and sweet in a wonderful way." Her song "Just the Way I Am" tries to explain this freedom of mind and spirit that other people can find difficult to understand.

Some of that comes from just living in the moment and letting go of inhibitions. She has been known to run around her property stark naked during a full moon (there she goes again!) without her wigs, her makeup, just her "little stubby self. Just God's little Dolly Parton again." She dances and twirls and feels the joy of being alive. You are never too old to chase fireflies and dance in the moonlight, and you don't even have to do it naked to have a good time! Try to be in the moment and appreciate the beauty around you. Where an adult will look at a puddle and see a nuisance to step around, a child will find great delight jumping in it and splashing.

If you are feeling too world-weary, try to see through the eyes of a child by spending time with them. Dolly said, "In my older years I'm going to go into that world of children. That's the way to keep yourself young. Be childlike, not childish." At age seventy-one, she released her first children's album, *I Believe in You*, and said she wrote many of the songs in the tree house and fairy palace that she had built on her property for her nieces and nephews. To write songs for children, she needed to go back and remember what it felt like to be that innocent and vulnerable.

Dolly sees being positive and happy as a personal responsibility, not only to herself but also to everyone else around her. She says, "If I am a shining light and people look up to me I'm very humble and grateful God has let me be a vehicle." With every new adventure, maintain your wonder and excitement.

WWDD TO CHOOSE HAPPINESS?

- Experience your feelings but don't get mired in the mud.
- Use dark times as a chance to evaluate your life and take inventory of what is working and what isn't. Then make the changes you need to develop resilience and bounce back.
- Live from your heart and a strong sense of purpose.
- Find your therapy.
- Be loving, not judgmental, toward yourself and others.
- Count your blessings, not your money.
- Don't take life too seriously and know how to have a good time.

Chapter Three

The Fairest of Them All

Have a Beauty and Style All Your Own

In the movie *Steel Magnolias*, Truvy, the small-town beautician played by Dolly, has a great line about there being no such thing as natural beauty. Dolly has said time and again that she wished she was pretty, because she always felt plain. She thought her natural hair was too thin and dishwater colored, her legs too short, and she hated her freckles. But look at any old photos of her, as far back as high school and even earlier, and they show she is naturally drop-dead gorgeous!

She always wanted pretty things, the kind of feminine trappings she didn't have growing up. The occasional Sears catalog was as close as she got to glamour. Her grandma used to give Avie Lee all of the prettiest flour sacks as fabric for Dolly's school dresses. Lacking access to makeup or cosmetics, for lipstick she used medicine cabinet antiseptics Merthiolate and Mercurochrome because they stained your skin red, flour as face powder to cover her freckles, pokeberries as rouge, burnt matchsticks as eyeliner, and honeysuckle as perfume.

As she became successful, her beauty routine evolved. Once she got to Nashville, she had real makeup for the first time and began crafting the Dolly Parton look as we know it. The fake eyelashes; the deep eyeshadow; the lined, glossy red lips; and the extra-long nails are all her trademarks, as well as her collection of many big, blond wigs. She became an expert in makeup application and used to tease all the other girls' hair in high school, although she made sure hers was always the highest. The over-the-top hair, makeup, and clothes fit her personality and certainly made her stand out, which was exactly the point.

Dolly has said if she wasn't a singer and musician, she would have opened a beauty shop. She feels she has to work hard to look good, and when she wakes up in the morning she has to "get up and paint on stuff." While wearing that much makeup may not be for everyone, there's certainly a lot we can learn from her self-assured approach to style and cultivating a memorable look.

"If I see something saggin', baggin', or draggin', I'm gonna have it nipped, tucked, or sucked!"

Use Style as Part of Your Brand

When in doubt, find your style mentor and emulate them until you eventually make your own. Dolly has told the story of her own inspiration so many times it has become part of her mythology. She even played the role in the autobiographical TV movie *Christmas of Many Colors*: "There was this one woman, I thought she was beautiful and, you know, she had the peroxide hair and she had it all piled up on her head and had red fingernails and red lipstick and, you know, wore her powder. And I just thought she was the prettiest thing I'd ever seen. And Mama said, Oh, quit looking at her. She ain't nothing but trash. And I thought, Ooh, that's what I want to be when I grow up—trash." She has also said that when she was a little girl, she liked the way the rich folks' wives dressed. She would see them driving around in their big cars all gussied up.

Dolly's famous image was deliberately created and continues to be maintained for a good reason. She wanted her outside to mirror her inside, which is, in a word, colorful. Your look, your image is also your brand. How you present yourself to the world makes a big impression, so make it a memorable one. It can mean the difference between being in the spotlight or out of it. Not everyone wants to look like Dolly or can pull it off. And it's probably not a look you want to wear to a conservative office. But don't be afraid to do something that stands out and fits your work and lifestyle, whether it's red lipstick or unique glasses. Whichever look you may be going for, you can always find someone who inspires you and emulate their style as best you can, whether it's Jackie Kennedy or Lady Gaga.

In Dolly's case it was an important part of standing out as a female singer: "I guess I did invent that part of me. I was always fascinated with fairytale images. Half of a show is the lighting and the shine and the sparkle. Stars are supposed to shine and maybe I just want to be a *star*."

While most of us would be hard-pressed to go full Dolly, unless we were in a Dolly Parton tribute band or drag contest, there are certainly things we can learn from her. It is also about accentuating your assets—and we all have them.

Dolly never leaves the house without her hair and makeup done—even for a quick trip to the grocery store. Not that she goes to the grocery store these days—she would create a riot. But even when she shows up for a 5:00 a.m. photo shoot where she will get full hair and makeup, she shows up in full hair and makeup. She says that she does it herself about 90 percent of the time, even though there are stylists and makeup artists on set. She has even said she will add more makeup or wash it all off and redo it if the makeup artist hasn't done her up enough. When in L.A. she sleeps with a wig on her nightstand, just in case there is an earthquake and she has to run out of the house in the middle of the night.

Your style conveys a powerful message about who you are and how people should treat you. The good news is that you get to choose what that message is. Jet-black hair, black lipstick, and nose rings send a message. So do jeans and T-shirts. So do pantsuits and sensible shoes. Or designer dresses and Louboutins. You get to decide what your uniform is and present your very best self to the world each day.

The Patron Saint of Drag Queens

"My image is two parts Diana Ross and Cher, one part David Bowie and three parts Dolly Parton, and that's how I came up with my persona."

—RuPaul

As a campy, vampy, curvy icon of exaggerated femininity, Dolly jokes that if she hadn't been born female, she would have ended up a drag queen. She once entered a drag queen look-alike contest—exaggerating her look—and lost. No one there realized they were going up against the real Dolly.

In an interview with Dolly and RuPaul, he said of her, "I think it's the fact that she uses her image as something so fun and so light. The music and the talent is so deep and so rich, with heartfelt emotions. I think the dichotomy of such a superficial image with such real, deep, heartfelt talent and emotion—that juxtaposition is what makes her so interesting."

Like so many drag queens, Dolly is all about projecting a fun, fabulous, confident image. It's about not taking yourself too seriously, knowing that talent and her groundedness are what make her so real and relatable.

There are countless Dolly look-alike contests, drag performances, and tribute bands all around the country: Night of 1000 Dollys in Nashville, Knoxville, and Toronto; Dollypalooza in New York, Brooklyn, and L.A.; Dollyween; the Dolly Should festival in Bay St. Louis, Mississippi; and tribute band Doll Parts, to name a few. Many of these events are fund-raisers with silent auctions and contests that raise money for her Imagination Library.

Dolly appreciates the tributes and at her shows she will sometimes sing "Jolene" with the slightly altered line, "Drag queen, please don't take my man."

Pretty Doesn't Happen All By Itself

Beauty is a process, and there is nothing like some primping and pampering to make a girl feel good. Dolly says she can get ready in about fifteen minutes, although she likes to have an hour. When you have the time, or for a special occasion, take a nice bubble bath, relax, meditate, and luxuriate in the rituals of beauty. It's the best of good old-fashioned "me" time.

Dolly mastered her own beauty rituals, starting with years spent experimenting with makeup. She has said, "I've used every makeup that's ever been on the market. If somebody at a makeup counter told me it was gonna make me gorgeous, I bought it." She is so into makeup that she made a deal with Revlon in 1993 to come out with her own Dolly

Parton's Beauty Confidence Makeup Collection that was sold via infomercials and even on Joan Rivers's *Can We Shop?* home shopping talk show.

The Beauty Confidence cosmetics included a twelve-piece makeup kit and a thirty-two-page instructional book showing Dolly applying makeup and sharing some of her dos, which include lying down for fifteen minutes with raw potato slices on your eyes to reduce puffiness and not applying blush too close to your eyes, which will only emphasize crow's-feet and under-eye circles and bags. Her message was to make the most of your own natural beauty and to pick your best feature—lips, eyes, cheeks—and play it up.

All Dolled Up

To get the full Dolly look, you need the wigs, the beaded and sequin clothes, the cleavage, the high platform shoes, the acrylic nails along with accessories, and, of course, the makeup. Dolly has employed varied looks throughout different eras—the 1960s, the '70s, the '80s, the '90s and aughts. One thing that has been pretty consistent over the years, however, is the way she paints on her face.

Alexis Michelle, who competed on Season 9 of *RuPaul's Drag Race*, won a lip-sync battle to Dolly's "Baby I'm Burning" on the show. As a professional makeup artist, in addition to being a talented performer, she offers the following tips to create your own Dolly beat:

1. Dolly loves pink tones, which work beautifully with her fair complexion. By building color to give a pigmented look, she creates a larger-than-life effect that works well on camera and on the concert stage and will stay put longer without washing out.

2. Apply a light nude creme or liquid, full-coverage foundation with a brush and swirl it in, or stipple/blend using a moistened and squeezed-out beauty blender for Dolly's trademark porcelain skin.

3. Use contouring cream or powder down the sides of the nose and a bright highlight down the center of the bridge to create the illusion of Dolly's narrow nose. Contour in a modified half-moon, almost like the Nike symbol, under the cheekbones to create Dolly-like apple cheeks. Apply highlight above this shape on the cheeks up to the lower eyelid and high up on the cheekbone.

4. Set foundation and contour with fair or neutral loose powder and a powder puff. Dust excess powder off with a large powder brush.

5. Using a medium brown eyebrow pencil or shadow, paint a strong, but fine, highly arched eyebrow by filling in your natural brow and lifting the arch slightly. Drag queens often use glue stick and other adhesives to cover their own eyebrows; once dry, they then cover with foundation and powder until they are no longer visible and then paint on a larger-than-life arch higher up on the forehead to really accent the eyes and feminize

the face. Depending on how well your natural brow compares to Dolly's, you might try this drag technique.

6. Apply a pale pink eyeshadow base from your upper lash line on the lids to under the brow bone. Then use a deeper, iridescent pink over that, focusing on the crease and the outer corners of the eyes, going all the way up and blending to under the brow bone.

7. Take a fine, angled eyeshadow brush to cut your crease with metallic cobalt blue, also focusing on the outside corners of each eyelid. Although it appears that Dolly is using purple eye shadow in many photos, it is in fact a lot of layers of pink with blue accents to create depth.

8. Use a third eyeshadow, in yet a darker shade of pink, to deepen the crease of the eye for dimension.

9. Finish the eyeshadow with an iridescent white or crème color under your brows, and at the inner corners of your eyes.

10. Using black liquid or crème-gel eyeliner, draw a thin, bold line along the top and bottom lash line. If you are going for a 1970s Dolly look, pull the eyeliner a little farther out the top lash line for a subtle cat eye.

11. Apply black mascara generously on both your top and bottom eyelashes and glue fake lashes along your top lash line.

12. Blend, blend, blend the contours and highlights in with a buffing brush or beauty blender to avoid hard lines. Dolly always looks soft and so should you.

13. Smile wide and brush a pale pink blush onto the apples of your cheeks, and up onto the cheekbones.

14. Using a pink or red lip liner, outline your lips going right to the edge of the lip line and even just beyond to achieve Dolly's exaggerated shape. Then color the whole lip in with the liner, and apply moisturizing lipstick or gloss in a rose, berry, or red on top.

15. Draw a tiny black mole on the left side of your chin, about an inch down and to the left of the corner of your mouth, with a dark brown, well-sharpened eyeliner pencil. Jet black will read too "Marilyn" and doesn't complement Dolly's soft and feminine coloring.

16. Now add a big blond wig, put on some extra-large hoop earrings and your push-up bra, and you are ready to go!

The Higher the Hair...

"People always ask me how long it takes to do my hair. I don't know. I'm never there."

Dolly decided early on in her career to wear wigs. That way she never has a bad hair day and can get ready in minutes. She says that when she was in high school, in the mid-sixties, bouffant hairdos became the big trend. Dolly's natural hair color is sandy blond and very fine, so when teasing started, she felt she had "just died and gone to heaven." She would tease and fix everyone's hair but claims hers was "the biggest hair in school." Why don't we doubt that? She says that when teasing started to go out of style, she never stopped, but over time it was damaging her hair.

She also complained that her hair is thin and so straight it doesn't hold a curl. Dolly wants curls—and lots of them, another reason she chooses to wear wigs. She says hers are cheap, synthetic, and not human hair or hand sewn. She even once sold her own line of Dolly Parton wigs through a full-color catalog. She has a cabinet on her tour bus that carries around five wigs so that they can be changed out and styled depending on her outfit or mood. When asked how many she has, she says, "At least 365, one for each day."

She used to travel with her hairdresser, Cheryl Riddle, who really was styling the wigs more than Dolly herself. Different wigs give you different feelings and she likes to have options, so if she doesn't like the first one she puts on, she can try on another. She says, "When I do my shows at night, there's a mood for my clothes and a mood for my hair. In the afternoon I think, 'I'm in the mood for white,' or 'I'm in the mood for red,' and then of course I think, 'Well, am I in the mood for curly hair or an updo?' So it all depends on my mood."

When she is at home, she doesn't wear wigs, just her own hair, sometimes up in a scrunchie. She dyes her hair to be the same blond color as the wigs, which she thinks is more radiant and shiny than her natural color. The key to get that Dolly look, either with a wig or on your own, is to make it big, with lots of volume and curls. That can be achieved with hot rollers, a teasing comb, and lots of hair spray. Or just go to Drybar and ask for the Southern Comfort with a little extra va-voom.

Learn the Tricks of the (Beauty) Trade

Once you've established your look, being able to get ready fast and efficiently is key. No one has hours every day to primp. Investing a little time and money up front can save you both on the back end.

It all starts with skin as clear as a mountain morning. Taking good care of your skin is the foundation for everything else. Dolly confesses that she often falls asleep in full makeup, which we all know is a big no-no and will clog your pores and leave your skin dull. But that must not always be the case, because in another interview, Dolly said, "I try all the new things that come out, but there's nothing better than good old Vaseline and those Almay eye makeup–remover pads. I use those little pads to clean my face and it leaves enough mineral oil on my skin that it's a good nighttime moisturizer. I have pretty good skin considering my age, and I think a lot of it is mineral oil and bacon grease." Dolly also has freckles and ran wild outdoors as a child, and rest assured that sunscreen was not on anyone's mind, as we now know it always should be.

Regular manicures and pedicures using bright nail polish, preferably a shade of red, is crucial. Dolly's long acrylic nails are a big part of her look. She has been known to use them as their own musical instrument, saying, "My nails are my rhythm section when I'm writing a song all alone. Someday, I may cut an album, just me and my nails." She even says that she came up with the rhythm for *9 to 5* on set using her nails on the back of her script. A contemporary look we think Dolly would appreciate is custom-made gel designs, which last for several weeks and can be a definite conversation starter or fashion statement. Imagine ten fingers, each with a black background and a tiny little musical instrument in white lacquer with itty-bitty crystals glued on. Eight nails could have each of the various instruments Dolly plays, and the remaining two could be musical notes or butterflies...but I digress. Obviously you need a professional to do this.

Dolly has bragged more than once that she can get ready in fifteen minutes, which is pretty impressive. While her makeup application may seem time-consuming—and she doesn't need to follow all the techniques of a drag queen since she already *is* Dolly—she has been doing it for so long that she can do it quickly. Wearing a wig that has been styled for you instead of having to blow-dry, curl, and tease your hair certainly saves a lot of time. But there are things you can do to make getting ready a snap—by having your beauty musts semi-permanent. Yes, it can be expensive and yes, you have to spend the time up front, but it pays off in the long run. You can safely get almost anything done in this day and age.

Dolly's eye makeup is quite elaborate, but it is the butterfly-like eyelashes that have the biggest impact. These can be achieved with a lot of mascara, with fake eyelashes, or with inserts and extensions. Extensions are professionally done, where a technician carefully glues additional eyelashes to your own to make lashes fuller and longer. They last several weeks and fall out much like your natural eyelashes. It can get expensive and it takes over an hour each time. But what a luxury to not have to wear mascara and to wake up looking so bright-eyed.

Dolly admits to nips and tucks, although she didn't come clean about it until she got caught by paparazzi coming out of her plastic surgeon's office. How else can you be over seventy and look like you're in your mid-forties? She certainly had a breast lift and augmentation, and maybe a tummy tuck, although she doesn't say. Beyond that she says she hasn't had a face-lift and would rather do two small tweaks every two years than "all of a sudden everybody knows you've had a face-lift. And you look so tight, like a banjo head."

As *Vogue* wrote in a piece that appeared after her seventy-first birthday, Dolly shows "no physical signs of aging either, a phenomenon she attributes to her weakness for injections." Dolly's youthful appearance is part of her job as an entertainer and she still has the voice and the energy to perform as she does, so why not nip and tuck and add volume where necessary? She says she hasn't had anything drastic done and prefers to get Botox and some fillers. Although she claims she will "never graduate from collagen," there are plenty of fillers that last anywhere from three months to two years.

Plastic surgeons and dermatologists alike are trained in doing this right so you don't end up with too much and looking puffy. Subtlety is key. And doctors are getting more and more subtle and giving "micro injections" to areas like lines around the upper lip, as the technology, and demand, keep growing.

She says that if it is going to make you feel good and you can afford it, go right ahead and do it, as long as you find the best doctors you can and communicate with them so you don't get "maimed or screwed up."

Like she says, "If you're my age you have got to do what you've got to do, especially on camera. I won't stop as long as I am living." She has also said, "My face pretty much maintains itself," which certainly sounds like a time saver and a blessing. Hallelujah!

"I think people give age too much importance. Old people who shine from inside look ten to twenty years younger."

Mysterious Body Art

Over the years, there have been many rumors and much discussion surrounding Dolly's tattoos. Some people say she always wears long sleeves because her arms and torso are covered with them. At one time she would let everyone wonder and not give a straight answer. After having a partial hysterectomy, she did tell gossip columnist Cindy Adams that she had keloid scars from the operation and that she was going to "get tattooed right over my stomach incision. I don't mean mermaids. I mean, from the left side of my navel down, I'll make what looks like a tiny ribbon of eyelet lace in very light colors. I'll make it baby pink. Baby lavender. With faint, tiny roses. I'll make a sweet delicate bow with what looks to be a little end that falls over like a piece of string…I'm going to tattoo cross stitches from one side to another. Like a bodice. It'll be very delicate. I sketched my design and already had a consultation with someone in New York who's going to do it for me…" With Dolly's vivid imagination and tendency to tell tall tales, who knows if she ever committed to such elaborate body art, but in other interviews she has said that she only had some small tattoos covering up her scars and that they were little butterflies and angels. Roseanne Barr said she had seen the tattoos and that she did indeed have beautiful little bows all over her body. More recently when she has been asked, Dolly has been more coy, saying she may have some but she sure isn't about to show them unless she gets caught.

No Rhinestone Unturned

There is no question that Dolly's clothing choices are a big part of her signature. An article in *Vogue* from 2015 discussed Dolly's fashion lessons, saying her outfits are "the embodiment of the character she's created, a real expression of individual, articulated, intentional style." As any girly-girl knows, dressing up can be a lot of fun. There are always special occasions when you want to stand out. Adding a little glitz when appropriate can make you feel like a star on your own stage.

Rhinestones, pearls, crystals, beading, embroidery, chiffon, sequins, fringe, leather pants, flowy sleeves, men's vests fitted tight with nothing underneath, sexy jumpsuits and rompers, jeans and high-heeled boots (of course!), denim button-downs tied at the waist, gingham with a twist, Western-style shirts with embroidered collars are all part of Dolly's "uniform." Some of this may be too much for most people but it does get her noticed.

Her elaborate platform heels are part of her trademark look. She wore Frederick's of Hollywood in her younger days and has many of her shoes custom made for her tiny feet (size 5.5); their tremendous height (five-inch heels) and elaborate designs match whatever outfit she is wearing with them, whether red, white, and blue stripes ready for the Fourth of July or pale aqua strappy platforms decorated with silver sequins and crystals for the Academy Awards. Some of the more elaborate ones were made by her 1980s designer, Tony Chase, others by Grisha and also Silvia's Costumes in L.A.

If you look at photos of Dolly from any era, you can't help but notice the big hoop earrings, bracelets, belly chains, and many elaborate filigree rings, shoes, scarves, and headbands. She has a ring made of diamonds and gold, shaped like a butterfly that is on ball bearings and flaps its wings. Many of her accessories match and coordinate with the outfit she is wearing. She doesn't just go for mix and match; she goes for an entire "look," one that is consistent where headbands, shoes, and handbags all match the dress.

Even her musical instruments are dressed up as accessories. At the Chasing Rainbows museum is an old wooden guitar with beautiful little birds, butterflies, and flowers painted in pastel blues and pinks all over it. And she has banjos, dulcimers, guitars, and harps that are a shiny, lacquered white and covered with Swarovski crystals. Treating a guitar as a piece of jewelry—100 percent Dolly!

It isn't just her accessories that she personalizes. There was a time, long ago, when she would buy clothes straight off the rack and then "Dollyize" them with a bedazzlement of rhinestones or sequins. Although with that exaggerated hourglass figure it's hard to imagine anything off the rack would actually fit her. Her current proportions are pretty impossible, between the low cuts, gigantic bosom, eighteen-inch waist, and skintight fit. Now her clothes are custom-made just for her.

We come in all shapes and sizes and off-the-rack doesn't always accommodate all body types. If you have a big chest like Dolly, you'll have to buy a size larger to fit your bosom and have the rest of it taken in. Since most of us don't have our own personal couture designers, get a good tailor—or a sewing machine if you have the skills—and fit your clothes to your individual proportions.

Dolly would never be trendy. She is, after all, one of a kind, a fine combination of burlap and satin. As Ms. Parton says, "I'd never stoop so low as to be fashionable. That's the easiest thing in the world to do." Find what makes you comfortable and makes you look good and don't be a mindless trend follower.

Dolly's Designers

Over her career, Dolly has had four major designers who worked with her to create beautiful, elaborate, one-of-a-kind clothing and stage costumes, shaping her image through over-the-top glamour. In the Chasing Rainbows museum, there are many, many of her gorgeous outfits on display where you can see the incredible creativity and handiwork of this talented group. They obviously follow the trends of the decade in which she wore them but they are all quintessential Dolly. She also has a refrigerated warehouse in Tennessee where she keeps close to 10,000 of her costumes and gowns, some of them weighing as much as thirty pounds with all the embellishments.

- Lucy Adams, a seamstress from Nashville, made all of Dolly's clothes for *The Porter Wagoner Show*, including her famous bell-bottom pantsuits from the early 1970s and the pink satin bell-sleeved dress with lace and rhinestones that she wore in 1970 in the parade for Dolly Parton Day in Sevierville, Tennessee. She worked with Dolly up until the time Dolly transitioned to Hollywood, and most of the outfits Dolly wears on her earlier album covers were designed by Lucy, and the two of them became and remained dear friends.

- Tony Chase designed Dolly's clothes and shoes in the 1980s and early '90s. His trademark was elaborate gowns with tons of sequins, beading, and pearls and took hundreds of hours of labor to make what was known as "couture for goddesses." He designed clothes and costumes for many celebrities but specifically women with curves, of which we know Dolly has many! He also wrote a book called *Fashion Therapy: A Revolutionary Program for Looking Your Best by Loving and Accepting Yourself*. He designed hundreds of stunning, richly detailed gowns, including the turquoise one Dolly wore to the 1990 Academy Awards (along with matching shoes and purse). Tony was very Hollywood, a dear friend, and known to have psychic abilities. His premature death from AIDS crushed Dolly and motivated her to devote much of her philanthropy toward AIDS research.

- Robert Behar started designing for Dolly when Tony passed away. He was a true French designer, quite elegant, and created some of her most beautiful stage clothes and gowns, including those she wore on both the red carpet and while performing at the Oscars the year she was nominated for her song "Travelin' Thru," which she wrote for *Transamerica*. She had been planning on just wearing costume jewelry because "I'm just a hillbilly" and he insisted that she wear real diamonds instead.

- Steve Summers currently designs and coordinates all of her clothes for TV, performances, and her own personal use and has taken on the title of creative director. He says, "My job as creative director requires me, obviously, to be relatively artistic, and as an artist, there is not a better canvas to work with. Dolly has so many sides to her personality that all require a specific look: I get Dolly the actress; I get Dolly the singer; I get Dolly the philanthropist; I get Dolly the book lady—I get all different kinds of Dollys. I get to dress them all and to dream up looks for each one." Steve originally worked at Dollywood as a dancer and singer and eventually got promoted because he was so creative and could do so many different things. Dolly says, "One day I was making some changes [and] he just popped in my mind like a light bulb. That was one of the best decisions I've ever made because Steve is fantastic with everything. He's so talented and so creative whether he's designing my clothes or making them. He's also a great decorator: He decorates all our places."

There is no denying that Dolly has an iconic one-of-a-kind style, one she deliberately created and that has evolved over the past fifty years with changing times and fashions. But she sticks to her basic principle that "everybody should look and be whatever makes them comfortable so their inner self—their God Light—can shine."

Of course your inner light can shine through without the need for glitz and glam. Perhaps the best beauty tip Parton has to offer comes from her character Truvy in *Steel Magnolias*: "Smile. It increases your face value."

WWDD TO MAKE HER BEAUTY STAND OUT?

- Think through the message you want your appearance to send and find a style mentor.
- Dare to be outrageously feminine.
- A girl should never leave the house "undone."
- Beauty is a process; learn and enjoy its rituals.
- Wear your hair according to your mood.
- Don't rule out antiaging or semipermanent procedures to streamline your prep time and look your best.
- Come up with a uniform suited to you and your lifestyle that makes you feel—and look—like a star on the stage of your own life.

Chapter Four

Backwoods Barbie

That Hourglass Figure

*F*amous for her killer curves, Dolly has spent a lifetime struggling with her weight and self-image. Despite her envious shape, she says she doesn't think of herself as sexy. She has said, "A lot of people get all turned off by the wig, the heels, the fingernails, the whole artificial bit."

She developed early, growing outward without growing vertically—she got curvy but stayed at a diminutive height. When she was thirteen, she looked like she was twenty-five. At twelve she had an old-school country baptism in the river. Her long white dress became transparent in the water and all of the boys who had gathered on the riverbank found religion for the first time, yelling, "Hallelujah!" Despite the disapproval from some of the church ladies, Dolly shrugged her shoulders and decided that God "wouldn't have given them to me if he didn't want people to notice."

She was unfairly judged as "fast," a designation that girls

who look older than their age have been assigned for millennia. It did embarrass her at first and she struggled throughout school, holding her head up high and maintaining her self-respect despite the false rumors that swirled around her. Over time she decided she might as well make herself look as good as she could and developed her flirty personality.

At five feet tall, her "fighting weight" is 100 to 110 pounds, but she has gone much higher and lower over the years. Her goal for her measurements: 40-20-36. That's a tough ratio to meet by any standards, but almost any woman can relate to her struggles with maintaining a healthy weight and figure. The difference is that being onstage, on television, and in the public eye, she feels the need to preserve a certain image. She decided she would have to view maintaining her figure as part of her job and approach it accordingly.

Over the years as her weight fluctuated up and down, she was forced to rethink her approach to eating, health, and weight maintenance. Now, in her seventies, she looks fabulous and seemingly immune from middle-age spread and beyond. And while she jokes that the steamer in her dressing room, used to de-wrinkle her clothes, is really a "jiffy suck" machine, beyond nips, tucks, and sucks, how did she do it? Let's find out!

"I tried every diet in the book. I tried some that weren't in the book. I tried eating the book. It tasted better than most of the diets."

That Magnificent Bosom

Dolly was always well developed, although being raised a religious country girl, she was quite modest. She might have worn her clothes tight but it wasn't until she became successful that she started to wear the low-cut outfits—or that her bosom "grew" in size and stature to become iconic and the source of many jokes. As her career continued, she started to use a familiar strategy and beat them to the punch with her own jokes since it got such a great reaction.

Johnny Carson famously lost his composure while interviewing her on *The Tonight Show* in 1977. After discussing her "zaftig" and "well-blessed" figure and discussing all of the Dolly Parton jokes she had to endure ("What's worse than a giraffe with a sore throat? Dolly Parton with a chest cold"), he famously said, "I have certain guidelines on this show but I would give about a year's pay to peek under there." Yes, it was a creepy comment that made her uncomfortable and one that wouldn't be tolerated today. She blushed and stammered at the time but the audience loved it.

She also says, "People always ask me if they're mine. Yes, they are—all bought and paid for." The reality is, she always had a large bust, even in high school and on *The Porter Wagoner Show*. At some point she had them lifted, most likely after her substantial weight loss when the rest of her got tinier and her bust got bigger. Those Barbie—or Dolly-like—proportions just don't happen in nature without some help.

And while I'm sure she was frustrated early in her career to have that be the focus instead of her tremendous talent, it has become part of the act. She says, "I'm a good sport. I know some of the best Dolly Parton jokes. I made 'em up myself."

"I walk tall. I got a tall attitude. But I'm just a little bitty person."

Don't Be Dietin' Dolly

Dolly is the first to admit that one of her biggest battles over the years was managing her weight. After a couple of decades of riding the dieting roller coaster, she finally decided to get off and be more sensible about her relationship with food.

When she was a little girl, she imagined that if she became rich and famous, it meant she could eat all of the cake and sweets and whatever else she wanted. You can't blame a girl for wanting to eat well after growing up on frog legs, catfish, and stone soup, among other more exotic things: "My father and my uncles were big bear hunters, and they had bear dogs. We ate a lot of bear, rabbit, squirrel and groundhog. See, we were country people, and when you grow up in the mountains you grow up eating whatever's running around."

Most of it was fried. She says she never even heard of shell-fish or oysters until she was well into her twenties. Having the world's most succulent and tasty foods available to you when you didn't even know they existed before, well, you're bound to go on a binge.

But that didn't happen until later. In the lean years of her early career, she had so little money for food and got so skinny her family was worried about her. She confesses to scouring the halls of hotels looking for leftovers on dis-carded room service trays and sometimes helping herself to food in the aisles of grocery stores.

She always had a gorgeous figure and then, she says, she got fat: "I didn't start to gain weight till I was rich and famous and started eatin' and eatin'. I'm a hog anyway, but I started cookin' on the bus, travelin' around, makin' nachos in the microwave, and just stoppin' at every truck stop." In her earlier days on the road, Dolly and the band would usu-ally stay at Howard Johnson's and, well, let's just say the food there isn't exactly healthy.

At one point while on tour she was restricted to a liquid protein diet. She went out with her band and crew and they were all eating fried clams and the delicious smell was kill-ing her. She tossed out her protein shake and ate the fried clams. In a fit of self-loathing, she said she was just going to give up and weigh 500 pounds and be buried in a piano case. That "all or nothing" dieting mind-set is a vicious cycle many women can relate to.

Not one to exercise, she has "endured every form of

torture anybody with a white coat and a clipboard could devise for a fat girl who really liked fried pork chops." She says she even took shots that she thought were made from cow pee in order to lose weight. Whether she was joking or not, we're not sure we want to know if that's true and we definitely don't want to try it!

During the filming of *9 to 5*, she felt that "my weight, of course, got to be a problem, because I'll be skinny, and then I'll go hog wild over something and put on 5 or 10 pounds, and with them all shooting the scenes out of order and all, I could walk in a door in the movie weighing one thing, and walk out of the same door weighing 10 pounds more." It's not necessarily noticeable watching the film today, but clearly she was self-conscious about her first big-screen appearance.

Getting onstage every night or in front of the camera every day in those tight-fitting, bedazzled, custom-made costumes puts a lot of pressure on a person. While most of us have our "fat pants" in case of emergency, if you're Dolly and traveling on a bus with just one small closet of clothing options, well, having them busting at the seams just isn't an option.

By her midthirties, all of her yo-yo dieting had started to take its toll on her metabolism and her health. Over a period of three years, she tried every imaginable diet and lost around fifty pounds. Dolly told Cindy Adams: "See, I'd always had this eating problem. I'd gain twenty pounds, lose it, gain it back the next week. In ten days, I'd put on ten pounds. On top of being sick and being medicated, Dietin'

Dolly would go on liquid protein, Scarsdale, Atkins, the water diet; then I'd binge, diet, gain, start all over again. Eventually my system wouldn't work anymore. My body couldn't hold up under that strain."

She spent a lot of that time starving herself and fasting, raising concern from her friends and family—and the media—that she had an eating disorder. Her rationale—whether it makes sense or not—was that she had to lose it all and then start fresh, so to speak, putting the pounds back on in a healthier way. But there was period of time when she looked like a "walkin' skeleton" and weighed as little as ninety pounds. Her husband, Carl, told her she was too skinny and Avie Lee started showing up cooking her good ole Southern comfort food to try to get some weight back on her.

> "Every single diet I ever fell off of was because of potatoes and gravy of some sort."

Dietin' Dolly

Some of Dolly's approaches to weight loss have been healthier and more effective than others. All of these extreme diets, combined with her rigorous performance schedule, caused her health to suffer. Who's to say whether or not she followed them under medical supervision, but either way, they aren't healthy and none of these are meant to be an ongoing way of life. These diets are sustainable only in the short run, if even that, and some are downright dangerous. Clearly, don't try any of these without talking to your doctor first.

Let's see how all of Dolly's various diets stack up:

Optifast: This is a medically supervised meal-replacement plan that lasts for twenty-six weeks. It consists of high-protein shakes, supplements, and added fiber; counseling; and lifestyle education. It is meant for people who need to lose a significant amount of weight. Dolly did it at UCLA, was monitored, and lost thirty pounds.

Liquid protein: This is a medically prescribed meal-replacement plan and is usually for pre- and post-bariatric surgery patients. It's not that much different from Optifast and requires a doctor's supervision.

Juice fast: There are many people who swear by the occasional juice fast as a way to jump-start weight loss and clear toxins from the body. There is a lot of debate about how healthy it actually is. There are many, many cold-pressed juice companies that offer juice fasts to go where you drink nothing but their juice—usually six bottles a day—for three to five days. Dolly probably did something called the Hollywood Diet, which is mostly fruit juices that adds up to consuming about 400 calories a day.

Water fast: This is just what it sounds like: eating no food and drinking only nine to thirteen glasses of water for three days. It is supposed to cut bloat, increase vigor and energy, and help the body detox, but it isn't safe for everyone—and might not be safe for anyone. If you drink too much water, it can mess up your electrolytes and cause hospitalization or even death.

The cabbage soup diet: This diet claims to be the go-to for whichever popular celebrity is in the spotlight at the time. At one time it was known as the "TWA diet," back when "stewardesses" had strict weight guidelines in order to keep their jobs. At some point, the tabloids claimed it was Dolly's preferred weight-loss method. When she heard about it she said, "I thought I might as well see if I can lose weight on my own diet." It consists of a homemade soup made of olive oil, chicken broth, celery, onion, bell peppers, carrots, tomatoes, and lots of cabbage. You eat nothing for seven days other than unlimited cabbage soup with the promise of losing ten pounds. It is low fat, high fiber, but there is no protein and it is missing a lot of nutrients. It also smells pretty bad and can have some traumatic effects on your digestive system! You will most likely gain the weight back as soon as you stop doing it.

The Stillman diet: This is a fourteen-day program that is also known as the "doctor's quick weight-loss diet." Named after Dr. Irwin Stillman, who created it, the diet is low carb and mostly low-fat protein. It promises dramatic and rapid weight loss and was the original high-protein, low-carb diet that paved the way for the others that are still popular today.

The Atkins diet: This is another popular version of a low-carb, high-protein diet but the difference is that it also includes high fat—think a lot of fatty red meat and bacon. This combination of controlling carbs and having high fat and high protein puts your body into ketosis, which eats away at your chub chub. The downside? It's definitely not vegetarian and causes bad breath.

The Scarsdale diet: This requires following an extremely regimented diet plan with specific foods for every meal for two weeks followed by two weeks of their trademarked "Keep Trim Eating Plan" with guaranteed weight loss. If, after the first month, you want to lose more weight, then go back to the original plan, alternating with the maintenance plan, for as long as you can stand it. Promising that you can lose one pound a day, it is pretty extreme and very low calorie.

The angel diet: The origins of this diet are uncertain but Dolly told Oprah on TV that when she sits and eats, she imagines God or angels are dining with her and she has to save some of the food on her plate for them. You don't want the angels to go hungry! I guess it's one way to manage portion control.

The Dolly Diet

In her autobiography, Dolly elaborates on how, after years of yo-yo dieting, she finally lost the weight for good and figured out a more balanced and sustainable approach to eating. It took many years for her to figure out that all those diets wouldn't work in the long run, so she created her own diet, which she calls "the Dolly Diet." This diet is a compromise that "Dolly the movie star was able to make with Dolly the pig that has kept both sides reasonably satisfied."

In 1984, she knew that change had to come from the inside out and set about creating a new lifestyle with habits that she could keep up despite her hardworking, hard traveling schedule. She came up with her own "conscious eating" program, which is about being aware of her own cravings, food issues, and triggers. One thing she is clear about is that she knows the Dolly Diet is not for everyone; it is just the diet for Dolly. It is purely what she has found works for her after many years of dieting extremes. While some of her weight-management techniques are a little unconventional (at least outside of Hollywood), some of them are just good ol' common sense.

The first step Dolly took when she developed her plan was to get educated about what food is good for her and what food isn't. When she was filming *Rhinestone*, she was finally ready to give up all of her strict diets and try a more sustainable approach. Working with Sylvester Stallone, who was extremely health-conscious, finally got her off the dieting roller coaster. He was shocked at the food she ate—like Velveeta and Wonder Bread, which are highly processed and have minimal nutritional value, food that isn't found in nature. He taught her about healthy eating and introduced her to his own low-carbohydrate, high-protein diet and had her eating just 1,000 calories a day. He also told her that she needed to work with health professionals, so she started meeting with nutritionists.

Sly and Dolly became weight-loss buddies during the filming, and having the support and extra motivation worked for both of them. He lost about forty pounds for the film and Dolly lost about twenty-five. At the start of filming, she was at about thirty or so pounds above her target weight of one hundred pounds.

From there she came up with a long-term eating plan based on her self-created individual awareness method (IAM). And while she has never laid out the specifics of her IAM approach, which seems to guide many aspects of her life, she does say that it is about being self-aware and doing what you know is going to work for you. In her autobiography, she wrote, "Overeatin' is as much a sickness as drugs or alcoholism. But you don't have to drink to live. You can stop drinking alcohol. You can stop all your habits. But you cannot stop eating. You have to eat to live." In other words, don't try to take on impossible diets you will never be able to maintain. Starving yourself doesn't work. Know thyself and work from there.

So how do we apply Dolly's philosophy to maintain our own figures? Understanding what your attitudes toward food are, determining why you're overindulging, and paying close attention to how you are feeling while you are eating is a start. Look inside yourself—you know yourself better than anyone else—and find your own solution. A diet only works if you are going to actually do it and stick to it.

Put simply, the plan is this: Eat better-quality food. Eat less. Eat six small meals a day. Be conscious of nutrition. Eat slower. Chew each mouthful longer. Think about what you are putting into your body. Satisfy your cravings—within reason. Consider eating healthy, low-carb foods Monday through Friday and go whole hog on the weekends. Once your body gets used to the healthier food, and once you see how much better you feel, you might not eat a gallon of ice cream and an entire platter of fried chicken or a whole pizza on Saturday night, even though you told yourself you can.

Now Dolly has a full-size refrigerator on her tour bus and keeps it full of low-carb, high-protein food packaged in Tupperware that her sister makes for her. The food is both healthy and, being in containers, portion controlled. She eats that during the week so she can eat what she wants on the weekends and holidays.

She has learned if you deprive yourself, you're just going to binge, so it's better to satisfy your cravings, in small doses. She told Cindy Adams in *Ladies' Home Journal*, "Before I consumed steak, potato, salad and dessert purely because it always went together. Today I try to *think* what I'm hungry for. I'll sit and look at it and think about the flavors. I'll think 'I'm really craving steak sauce. And potato. I don't really want meat or salad.' So I'll put steak sauce on the potato and eat that. If what I really want is dessert I'll tell the waiter, 'I'm dieting and would like to take this food home and eat it for lunch,' which is my big meal. Then I'll order chocolate mousse while the others eat dinner. While they're on dessert I'll have black Sanka. It used to be coffee with cream and sugar." Dolly still eats biscuits and gravy, fried chicken, and all of her other favorite foods; she just eats them on the weekends and eats less of them.

She also doesn't want the people around her to feel bad, especially since she is traveling so much and eating in restaurants with friends, bandmates, journalists, and business associates. If she wants to order six dishes of different foods, she will do it (and she can afford it!), but she will eat only a bite of each. This way she fixes her cravings and no one around her feels sorry for her. And her dinner mates get to eat the leftovers. Ordering six entrees in a restaurant and eating only one bite of each sounds crazy to most people, to say nothing of wasteful. Her point is that it works for her. This is *her* approach.

In one interview she said, "Our taste buds are all in our mouths. Once we swallow, we don't really taste the food. The pleasure and satisfaction is in the tasting and chewing." Instead of inhaling her food, she slows down and chews it thoroughly. And apparently sometimes Dolly, and a lot of other celebrities who have to be extremely weight conscious, will chew their food and then spit it out. Not throwing it up, mind you. Just never swallowing it to begin with. It sounds a little gross and borderline eating disorder, but I guess if you're not spitting your food out in front of anyone and carry a spittoon with you—and I'm not saying that Dolly does—this could work. It's one way to have your cake and not eat it too.

Dolly Parton Basic Training

Dolly has never been one to work out and claims to hate exercise. Despite that, there have been times when she has tried various activities in an effort to get into shape.

After Sly Stallone helped her clean up her junk food diet, he talked the exercise-phobic Dolly into weight training to help her get into shape. This was a woman who had never exercised or been an athlete, never wore tennis shoes (it's hard to do knee raises or squats in high heels), and used to joke that her friend Jane Fonda's videotapes were too hard for her and that she ended up on the couch, watching them while eating cookies.

In her late thirties, inspired by Stallone, she installed a gym in her home in Los Angeles and got two weeks of private training from a top-notch Hollywood bodybuilder to help her get started. They would start with twenty minutes of stretching and then move on to some very basic general toning exercises: toe touches, knee bends, side twists, and knee raises; abdominal exercises like leg scissors, bicycles, and sit-ups with elbows going to knees; and cardio exercises like jumping in place. All of this was meant to build up her stamina so she could then take it to the next step.

At one extremely optimistic point, she said, "I have a three month basic-training program in mind." She also said she was going to turn her Nashville farm into a training ground, "like a military camp where there's no choice. You have to learn. After I determine how long it takes to put a body into shape, I'll organize a follow up maintenance program. If this works for me I'm going to set up Dolly Parton Basic Training Centers. My centers will teach the spiritual part of fitness, including meditation. The method will be mind-body-soul discipline." While the basic training centers never came to fruition, Dolly looks as fit as a fiddle, so whatever she is doing, it seems to be working.

Just as she had created a healthier eating program for herself, she created a personalized exercise regime. She found activities she felt she could do, have fun, and stick with. These included yoga, dancing, karate, mini-trampoline jumping, weight training, and boot camp–style routines. There's a terrific old black-and-white photo of her holding small dumbbells with a mini-trampoline in front of her. She even traveled with the trampoline and would keep it with her at the Chateau Marmont when she was filming in L.A.

She also loves hiking in the woods or around the lake by her house. And she plays the occasional game of tennis or round of golf or goes for a swim, proving you don't have to be a gym rat in order to stay in shape.

WWDD TO MAINTAIN HER IDEAL WEIGHT?

- Crash diets and yo-yo dieting will hurt your health—get off the dieting roller coaster.
- Change your attitude toward food—know your cravings, your food issues, and your triggers and find a way to eat that you will stick with for a lifetime.
- Eat less, and eat for nutrition and health.
- But don't deprive yourself; go ahead and satisfy the occasional craving.
- Find exercise that you enjoy and will stick with.

Chapter Five

Men Are My Weakness

Love and Marriage

Dolly has said she never met a man she didn't like and even wrote a song by that name. I would venture to say there isn't a man Dolly has met who didn't like *her*. Men have been known to break into spontaneous applause when she walks into a room, as witnessed during an interview with the *New York Times* in 1992. A group of serious-looking men, huddled together in conversation, stopped and stood up in a standing ovation when she walked into the Midtown Manhattan restaurant Wally's and Joseph's.

Dolly's combination of beauty, charm, and flirtatiousness, along with her talent and brains, have left many a broken heart in her wake. Dolly and Merle Haggard toured together in the mid-'70s, and Merle said in a 1981 magazine article and his 2002 memoir that he had both strong feelings and an attraction to her. He wrote his 1975 song "Always Wanting

You," which became a number one hit, about his unrequited love for her. Never mind that he was married at the time. He has called her "the most charismatic human being alive. She's Marilyn Monroe with a guitar."

As a kid, Dolly was a tomboy and ran around barefoot, playing and fighting with boys and girls alike. But once she got older, she developed a bit of a reputation, one that she didn't deserve. There's always that one girl who, just by virtue of being gorgeous or an early developer, has everyone talking and the rumors start flying. She told Chet Flippo at *Rolling Stone*, "Well, I tell you, it was kinda rough for me because I was the most popular girl in school in the *wrong* way. *Everybody* talked about Dolly but I didn't have as many friends as I should have had. My best friends were boys because they understood me and weren't tryin' to find fault."

She says that she didn't date the boys in school because she felt so much older than them, she was a lot more mature, and, well, she had that body by the time she was thirteen. She said she felt a bit like their mother. That doesn't mean they didn't try or that she didn't enjoy their admiration. She would sit in the last pew in church and the boys would come and throw rocks or scratch at the window trying to get her attention. And sometimes, one lucky guy would get to walk her home.

Her appeal to the male species has continued throughout her life. There is that curvy figure and the tight clothes and high heels, big blond hair, creamy skin, and ready smile, but her appeal is more than the exaggerated femininity. So much of her beauty comes from within, from her boundless, positive energy, her intelligence, her fierce spirit, her bawdiness and wit.

Also, she's an incorrigible flirt.

Despite the endless tabloid stories over the years of her many supposed lovers—including Burt Reynolds and her best friend, Judy Ogle—she has been married to Carl Dean for over fifty-one years. She said in *The Dolly Parton Scrapbook*, as well as in *Newsweek*, "I need my husband for the love, and other men for my work. But I don't depend on any man for my strength." You got that right, girl!

> "When I talk to a man, I can always tell what he's thinking by where he's looking. If he's looking at my eyes, he's looking for intelligence. If he's looking at my mouth, he's looking for wisdom. If he's looking anywhere except my chest, he's looking for another man."

Honky-Tonk Angel

Dolly flirts with everyone, including journalists who interview her and her audience: "I love to flirt . . . men are my weakness. Short, fat, bald or skinny." Growing up around so many men—her father, uncles, and brothers—she always felt that she understood them and they didn't scare her. As a teenager, she would drive around with a girlfriend and cruise the local

Tastee-Freez, shouting out at the boys from the car window, telling jokes and playing her guitar to get their attention.

Her techniques are pretty standard but also effective: flashing dimples, giggling, playful banter, teasing, and flattery. Walking into a room of male journalists for a press event, she'll say something nice about each one or appeal to their ego: "My you're a big one, aren't you?" or "Aren't *you* sweet?!" In one TV interview promoting her DreamMore resort, when the anchor said he might go get a room there, she replied, "I might stay there with you." Nothing like getting a serious newsman to blush on national television. It's all in good fun and mostly harmless. A good flirt can be playful with men or women, and age is irrelevant. It's really about giving special attention to someone to break the ice or get a laugh. And typically, people leave her presence smitten.

Sometimes the crushes are mutual: "I've had crushes on some very unusual men...and I'm not having sex with these people—I'm just flirtin' and having fun." And, yes, she has been married a long time, but as she says, "That's not to say I'm blind or dead." Keeping that sense of being attractive—and attracted—keeps you having fun and feeling alive, whether you are otherwise committed or not. As long as you know your boundaries.

Beyond being playful and a flirt, Dolly also knows how to lay on the charm when necessary. When she walked onto the set of *9 to 5* for the first time, she was a newbie, the inexperienced hick showing up for her first movie. The powers-that-be weren't sure what to expect from her and the more experienced Hollywood types thought that given her appearance and her country girl background, the (mostly male) crew would be disrespectful or make jokes about her. She walked on set with a big smile and made a self-deprecating joke and within seconds had the entire crew on her side. Whatever their preconceived notions of her were, she disarmed them in an instant with a few words. And in short order, her professionalism demanded their respect. Nashville radio DJ Ralph Emery, who has interviewed her many times, says she has "the brains of a computer, the heart of an artist and the spirit of a minister." It takes intelligence, an understanding of how other people think, and a sort of blind confidence to charm a tough audience.

Part of being able to disarm others with charm is maintaining a degree of mystery. It throws people off balance. Jane Fonda, her costar in *9 to 5*, said of her, "Very often someone will wow you, but as you get to know them, the mystery wears off. One of the things that just flabbergasts me about Dolly is the amount of mystery she has." Sylvester Stallone said of her, "What you see is only a subtle representative of what she is. Not that I know firsthand, but Dolly always holds something back in reserve. She is an incredible woman."

Of course men, being visual creatures, will always be dazzled by beauty. Whether a born beauty or a self-made bombshell, it gets the boys' attention. She received many "love letters" in high school, including one from a classmate who apologized for being jealous but said he couldn't help it—she was just so darn pretty. Whatever the backstory on that one is, she was clearly turning heads from an early age. Even if this is politically incorrect, men know what they find attractive the minute they see it, so playing and dressing up your more feminine features is never gonna hurt.

Say Forever You'll be Mine

She met her husband, Carl Dean, on her first day in Nashville. She was just eighteen years old and had been in such a hurry to get to town that she had packed little other than a bag full of dirty laundry. She was walking outside the Wishy-Washy Laundromat drinking a Coca-Cola when a cute boy in a truck drove by and hollered out the window at her. She hollered back. He circled around and got out of his truck, and they started talking. The attraction was mutual and instant. Dolly said that as soon as she met Carl, there was no point in looking for anybody else. She had left two boyfriends back home to go pursue her career and wasn't looking for any distractions. But Carl proved to be irresistible.

Carl Dean had grown up in Nashville, and he and his father had an asphalt paving business. He was a tall drink of water—dark haired and handsome. He has been described as Lincolnesque, but pictures prove him much better-looking. He can be reserved but has a wicked sense of humor when he feels comfortable among people he knows. Dolly has said he is one of the smartest men she has ever met and that, like her daddy, he has good old-fashioned horse sense.

That first week they met, he would visit her while she baby-sat her nephew, Uncle Bill's son, but she never let him inside the house; they just sat on the porch and talked and talked, getting to know each other. When they finally had a real date a week or so later, he took her straight to his mother's house for supper and introduced her to his family. Any boy who takes you to his mother's house on your first date is a keeper.

When Dolly and Carl originally got married, they had to do it on the sly because her managers and record label peo-ple thought it would kill her budding career. They ran off to the small town of Ringgold, Georgia, and got married, he in a suit and she in a simple white dress her mother had made, with no one in attendance other than the preacher and his wife. They managed to keep it a secret for a year or two.

In interview after interview, she has said they have a very happy marriage and will always love each other despite her being on the road most of the year. He gives her the freedom she craves and she lets him stay out of the limelight.

Dolly's Rules for a Happy Marriage

- **R-E-S-P-E-C-T:** It's true of all relationships—you have to respect each other. Dolly says, "My husband is a very accepting person of me. That's his best quality. He lets me be me." She, in turn, respects and accepts him and his homebody, low-key ways. She can count on him. As she says, "He's my anchor and I'm his excitement."

- **Have a sense of humor:** Make each other laugh. Both Dolly and Carl have a penchant for making mischief and playing tricks on people and each other. It keeps them both entertained. Dolly tells a funny story about the time that Carl came and visited the set of *9 to 5*: "He is very good-looking and very magnetic and women are really taken with him. I was sitting with Jane Fonda, talking about the kind of men we think are good-looking. So we look across the stage and there's Carl. And Jane says: 'Now that's my kinda man.' She looks at me and says: 'I saw him first!' A few minutes later she kinda sidles over and she finds out it's Carl, my husband. She was so embarrassed!" Dolly knew that Carl would get a total kick out of it, so why not let him have his moment? And I'm sure they all got a good laugh out of it.

- **Be friends first and foremost:** Carl knew Dolly before she became a star and saw her struggles to get to where she is. She doesn't have to worry about him loving her for her money or her stardom. He loves her today for the same reasons he loved her the first day they met. She has said, "We're good friends first of all...He's very kind, very understanding, crazy, funny, witty." Truly seeing each other for who they are and not only tolerating each other's differences but also loving each other in spite of them is the best foundation for a healthy marriage and a friendship.

- **Maintain your independence:** When Dolly moved to Nashville, she didn't want to get involved with anyone because she was there to focus on her music. "I didn't want to get married. All I had ever known was housework and kids and workin' in the fields. But I didn't want to be domestic; I wanted to be *free*." She didn't think it was going to happen because what man would want to marry someone who was going to be traveling around and pursuing her own dreams rather than being a traditional wife at home? Carl clearly met her requirements. "See, Carl gives me what no one else can: the freedom to work. My husband is happy to let me fly."

One of the reasons she decided to marry him and one of the major reasons that the marriage has lasted as long as it has is that he supports her traveling around the country performing and working and encourages her rather than holding her back. He doesn't need her home putting dinner on the table; he knows how to cook himself. And while Dolly is a terrific cook when she is home, her domestic duties are for her own pleasure, not just more work for her.

She didn't take Carl's last name when she got married in the 1960s, which was pretty unconventional at that time. She said that the name on her passport is Dolly Parton Dean but that "I didn't change my name publicly because I already had a record deal. It made no sense. He never asked me to."

Carl is not involved in her career at all, unlike so many of her female peers who had their husbands functioning as their managers. Dolly doesn't mix marriage and career and says she has nerves of steel but that her nerves couldn't handle a husband who was trying to run her business. She thinks it would just mess everything up.

- **Spend time apart:** Carl is an incredibly private person and doesn't like large groups of people or a lot of fuss. It has been said that "to Carl, three's a crowd and four's a mob." They're very different but they give each other space. And it works for them. Being secure enough in your relationship to go off and do what you enjoy professionally or socially will prevent things from getting stale.

Early on in Dolly's career, she won Song of the Year and she asked Carl to go with her to the ceremony. She had him dress up in a tux and accompany her while she hobnobbed with industry folk. He was proud of her but hated every minute and afterward told her, "Now, I want you to do everything you want to do. I want you to enjoy every minute of your life. But don't you ever ask me to go to another one of these things." That experience established the tone and pattern for their marriage.

Giving each other plenty of space and respecting each other's need to do their own thing is an important part of their compatibility. She says that he lets her be married and single at the same time, which just means he is okay that she goes off and pursues her own career and interests. He isn't jealous or competitive or suspicious. That can still be unusual in this day and age, but back in the late 1960s it was almost unheard of.

- **Keep it fresh**: Spending a lot of time apart pretty much guarantees they'll never get sick of each other and gives them time to miss each other. But they make sure to do considerate things and to show each other appreciation. Dolly says that Carl "always makes me feel pretty, even when I'm not. I think Carl will always see me the way he did when we first met, just as I do him. We'll never be old to each other." He picks flowers for her, makes her coffee in the morning, and is generally thoughtful. She tries to do the same sorts of loving things for him.

- **Stick it out through thick and thin**: Dolly saw her parents' marriage as a model, if an imperfect one. Despite poverty, all of those children, lots of drinking (his), overwork (for both of them), his occasional disappearances, and other ups and downs, they stuck together. Her view is, "Well, there's no perfect marriage, and, no, I've never thought about packing it in. I just kick his ass and go on the road. Or, he'll kick mine and go to the barn."

- **Have a healthy attitude toward sex**: Dolly keeps her sex life private, but the affection they have for each other and their playful and open personalities indicates a satisfying sex life. She says she has always been curious and open-minded about sex and that she loves it and has never had a bad experience: "I am a very emotional person and to me it's another way, a very intimate and wonderful way, of showing emotion. It has never been dirty to me."

- **Celebrate your union:** For years, until the Wishy-Washy Laundromat closed, every year on their anniversary Dolly and Carl would get some Krystal Burgers to go, and eat them at the place where they first met. For their Golden Anniversary, Dolly not only wrote the album *Pure & Simple* as a celebration of their long marriage but also wanted to have the big, fancy wedding she couldn't have the first time around. She wore the long beaded wedding gown she always wanted and made Carl put on a tux, just that once. They had a ceremony in the chapel on their property and then took the RV back to Ringgold and spent the night where they had their wedding night fifty years before.

Who was Jolene?

There has been a lot of speculation about Dolly's famous song "Jolene" about a beautiful red-haired woman trying to take her man. So many journalists have interpreted the song to mean that her marriage was in jeopardy that in recent interviews Dolly has told how she came to write the song. Given the punch line, it is surely one of her tall tales: "My husband was flirting with this redheaded girl at the bank," she says. "My husband appreciates and loves pretty women and I was just jealous because she was tall and beautiful. Nothing ever happened. But we didn't bank there anymore. Too much interest going on at that bank!"

In reality, the song was inspired by a little girl Dolly met whose name was Jolene. She was a young fan with red hair, pale skin, and beautiful green eyes. Dolly asked her whether or not she was named after her father, who she assumed must be named Joe. The girl said no, she was just Jolene. Dolly thought it was such a pretty and unusual name that she wanted to write a song about a woman with that name and just started saying "Jolene, Jolene, Jolene, Jolene" to herself and it started to have its own rhythm and a song was born. Not only has it become a sing-along song at her concerts and on jukeboxes everywhere, but it has also been performed and recorded with very different arrangements by a variety of artists, including Miley Cyrus, the White Stripes, Pentatonix, and even Olivia Newton-John.

Love Is Like a Butterfly

Dolly says that Carl is without question her greatest love, but she also admits that she has known some other great loves throughout her life. This doesn't mean she is necessarily having affairs involving a sexual relationship. For her it includes her many friendships with men, whether her collaborators, like Porter Wagoner, or her former bandleader and confidant, Gregg Perry, and many more. Yes, you can be close friends with members of the opposite sex.

She has said that Kenny Rogers has been one of the great loves of her life: "It was never romantic, but it was passionate and loving." They have both said that they had fun with all the rumors of their supposed affair but that it never actually happened. "We could've gone down that road. And a lot of people do. And we probably *have* with other people. But Kenny's like a brother to me...I just never thought of him that way...I liked him too much. That would screw up everything."

Whatever she has or has not done, Dolly is always going to have flirtations but she is clear that a flirtation is not the same as an affair and that Carl "knows I'm always coming home."

Her unconventional way of speaking about all of these loves has led to constant references to her having an "open marriage." She says she does not and told Oprah in an interview, "I have many wonderful relationships with men and women that are love affairs of a sort. I mean, sex and love are two different things." This appreciation of love in all of its forms is what she must mean when she sings about the "multi-colored moods of love." She knew this well before bromances and girl crushes became part of the vernacular.

Her definition of an "open marriage" is her own and "just means we let each other be who we are and how we are. He knows I'm a flirt and a tease, but it's harmless. I've never met the man that would take his place." There has been a long-standing rumor that because she travels so much, she and Carl have only spent a total of six months together over the course of their entire marriage, which she says is not only untrue but also cruel. Carl often joins her on the road or comes and stays with her in L.A. or wherever she might be; he just does it quietly and keeps a low profile. She keeps him out of the public eye because that's the way he wants it.

When asked how she can write so many songs about love and always be finding new angles on it, she says, "Love is always growing, and we grow as people as well, so you just automatically take on new twists and turns." Some people mistakenly believe that her songs about love, in all of its forms, are based on her own experience. Her song "Can't Be That Wrong" is what she calls the "ultimate cheating song," but she kept rewriting it because she didn't want her fans to think it was about her.

The reality is that Dolly is an artist, an insightful observer of human nature, and she doesn't need to experience something firsthand in order to write about it. Given her incredible life, she has witnessed all sorts of love around her, whether in her family or friendships or career.

"I'm Sixteen" is about one of her sisters, who had given up on love and then fell hard at age sixty and how she felt like a teenager again.

She has been called the "Queen of the Tabloids," and the subject of relentless rumors and untruths. Over the years, she has been accused of being involved with every man she has ever worked with. Just like she was accused of messing around with all the boys in high school. Some of the coverage is more outrageous than others. Many years ago, she appeared on the cover of *Woman's World* with a headline promising an "exclusive" on why her husband has to pay to see her. Carl hasn't been photographed in many years, and some people have questioned whether he really exists (he does). Some tabloids have claimed that she and her best friend, Judy, are lesbian lovers (they're not). All sorts of outrageous things have been said about her, but she doesn't respond and has come up with a self-deprecating, evasive response to address the rumors, which means no one really knows what is true and what is not: "Maybe I have, maybe I ain't. I never tell if I have."

Various tabloids, mistakenly believing they caught Carl on film, have run photos of her with her bus driver, gardener, and hairdresser. He is so rarely photographed that they think any unidentifiable mystery man is her elusive husband. Or they have said that he is made up and doesn't exist at all! And of course, because she is photographed with her costars at various premieres and events, these publications all claim she must be dating them or having an affair.

In spite of all this, keeping their marriage private has helped them keep their marriage strong and they try to find the humor in the endless stories. In one photo Carl, in his goofy way, posed with Dolly with a paper bag over his head, just to play with all of the silly rumors Ms. Dolly prefers to keep everyone guessing: "I don't deny or admit anything for sure. I'd rather be thought of as passionate and exciting

than as some vanilla person who's never done anything...
I've enjoyed every rumor."

During the filming of *The Best Little Whorehouse in Texas*,
a story spread that she and Burt Reynolds were having an
affair. In fact, Dolly has revealed more than once that Burt was
moody and difficult on set and was going through a tough time
after breaking up with the love of his life, Sally Field. Still, she
and Carl had some fun with the tabloid reports. She tells the
story of being home one day, playing with their Boston terrier,
Popeye, wrapping him in a blanket and carrying him like a
baby. Carl took a picture and said, "Here. I want you to send
this to the *National Enquirer* and tell 'em that this is a picture
of your and Burt's baby." They had a good laugh over that one.

Being solid in your love for each other and understanding what the other needs in order to be happy goes a long
way toward maintaining a long-term bond. And everyone
doesn't need to know your business. You have to rise above
what others think or say about your relationship and keep
it between the two of you. And find humor in other people's
expectations of what your relationship should look like.

Of course, having crushes and flirtations can sometimes
create a tricky situation where either you or the object of
your attention can get the wrong idea. And given the reaction she creates in men, there were certainly times in her
career when she had to deal with uncomfortable situations.
She has said, "I have an open heart and an open mind and
sometimes I talk too much and I'm joking and people take it
the way they want to hear it."

Dolly claims that few men in a business environment ever seriously tried to put the moves on her. As she became more famous and powerful, one has to think that she intimidated them a bit. She says, "If I see somebody I'm fascinated by, we will share a kind of relationship through conversation, through whatever we feel is necessary, but it's always plain there's Carl, the one man I want to grow old with."

Dolly has always been pretty straightforward with the men who took a flirtation too far without hurting their pride, whether with honesty, a harmless zinger or joke, or a reference to her—or his—spouse. A few firm words could put them in their place.

If worst comes to worst and none of those techniques work, you can always do what Dolly did on one of her first trips to New York when she was just twenty-three. In 1969, Dolly and Judy went to New York City for the first time. They were dressed up with "gaudy hair" and walking around the gritty streets near 42nd Street and Times Square, decades before it became the chain store tourist trap it is today. One guy followed them and kept making comments and grabbed her, refusing to leave her alone. She said, "Back then, I was just a country girl, and my father had given me a gun to take with me to New York. So I had to tell this guy that if he didn't stop touching me, I'd turn him from a rooster into a hen. That's where that line [from the movie 9 to 5] comes from."

Well, I guess that's one way to deal with someone who won't take no for an answer.

WWDD IN HER RELATIONSHIPS WITH MEN?

- Be a flirt, disarm them with charm, and dazzle them with beauty.
- When you find the love of your life, whether you are looking or not, go all in.
- Love comes in many forms and doesn't need to be sexual.
- Close friendship with the opposite sex is not only possible but also desirable, as long as your boundaries are clear.
- Create a marriage that works for the two of you and your shared values and interests.
- Maintain your privacy; you don't need to answer to anyone else when it comes to your relationship.

Chapter Six

Blond Ambition

Money and Business

*D*olly may seem frivolous on the outside, but she is dead serious when it comes to music and business. Danny Nozell, the CEO of CTK Management and Dolly Records, says, "I wish some of the younger entertainers would take some lessons from Dolly because she is the most professional person. Is she tough? Absolutely she is. Behind closed doors, the gloves come off and the nails come out. At the same time, she's the sweetest, nicest person I've ever met. But she's a very hardcore businesswoman."

In 2016 the BBC interviewed Dolly and said she was a "honky-tonk version of the Ginger Rogers adage, doing everything her male counterparts do, but backwards and in rhinestones." Ain't that the truth.

In the world of country music, she was a trailblazer. Her only female predecessors were Kitty Wells and Patsy Cline, who both looked and dressed in traditional country music style. There weren't many women in country music outside of the "girl singer" sidekick. The industry was so prejudiced against women in the 1960s when Dolly was starting out that, according to music journalist Robert Oermann, you had to be twice as good as a man to get noticed. But Dolly was no dumb blonde and understood men and how they think, having grown up among so many brothers, uncles, cousins, and her father. The male establishment didn't scare her and she felt that being a woman served her well. They couldn't see beyond her appearance and underestimated her abilities and drive, which she used to her advantage. She was a bit of a secret subversive.

In 1977, she told biographer and music journalist Alanna Nash, "I'm not going to limit myself just because people won't accept the fact that I can do something else." Nash's interpretation was that she was not the first country giant to pursue a career that crossed over into the mainstream but that she *was* the first established female country star to do it, and the men of the Nashville old boys' club objected to her move because they "want 'their' women to stay where they've always been."

So how can you get your stiletto—or boot—through the door and then kick it open? Sometimes, like Dolly, you just have to build your own door.

> "I have looked up at a glass ceiling, and thrown one of my five-inch high heels and smashed right through it."

Dolly, Inc.

Dolly has been reported to be worth over $650 million and helms an empire that includes successful businesses across industries.

Music: Since early in her career, she kept the rights to her publishing catalog of songs, which earns her millions in royalties. She's made 80 albums, had 25 number one singles, sold more than 100 million albums, had 115 singles on the charts, and published more than 3,000 of her own songs. She produces and releases her music on her own record labels—Blue Eye Records and now Dolly Records.

Film/television: In addition to being a successful and beloved actress in movies like *9 to 5*, *Steel Magnolias*, and *Joyful Noise* and a guest on TV shows like *Hannah Montana*, she has owned several production companies over the years. She started Sandollar Productions with Sandy Gallin, which coproduced the wildly successful television series *Buffy the Vampire Slayer* and its spinoff, *Angel*.

She also has a development deal with NBCUniversal with production company Magnolia Hill. The first picture, *Coat of Many Colors*, aired in December 2016, drawing more than 13 million live viewers, making it the most viewed film on broadcast TV in over five years, and was nominated for an Emmy. With its success she produced and had a role in *Christmas of Many Colors*, with plans to create shows based on some of her other songs. She has also created and produced shows for Netflix, Country Music Television, and other outlets.

Real estate: In addition to her Brentwood, Tennessee, estate; a nearby lake house; a "city house" in Nashville; her office complex; and her Tennessee Mountain home where she grew up (which has become a tourist attraction), she has or had homes around Los Angeles, New York, and at one time Hawaii.

Dollywood: The Pigeon Forge–based Dollywood theme park and the Splash Country water park has 3 million visitors a year. Working with Herschend Family Entertainment, they partnered to start the Dollywood Company, which also has three dinner theater restaurants, Dolly Parton's Stampede, Smoky Mountain Adventures, and Pirate Adventure. Her initial $6 million investment in Dollywood now brings in $30 million a year.

Lodging: She has vacation cabin rentals in the Smoky Mountains and in 2015 she opened her 307-room DreamMore Resort near Dollywood.

Authorship: She has written several books, including her two memoirs, *Dolly: My Life and Other Unfinished Business* and *Dream More*; her cookbook *Dolly's Dixie Fixin's*; and two children's books, *I Am a Rainbow* and *Coat of Many Colors*.

Other businesses: Cosmetics, wigs, macadamia trees, farm equipment, hardware stores, and garden centers.

Dang! All this from a little girl who grew up in the hollers of eastern Tennessee in a shack with no running water.

"I've made a fortune looking cheap, but I'm nobody's fool. When I was starting out, people didn't take me seriously. I always looked like I could be had, but the truth was, I couldn't."

Be a "Professionalist"

There are plenty of people out there who do just enough to get by or who are just going through the motions. Dolly refuses to accept that kind of mediocrity or complacency and calls herself a "professionalist"—a word she created that combines *professional* with *perfectionist*. Dolly said that one of the missions of her Dollywood Foundation is to help people care more, and by that she means care about how you look, how you prepare, and how you keep your commitments and to always be striving to be the best you can be. She once told *Southern Living*, "I ain't all that smart, to be honest. I'm just smart about what I know. I'm a very professional Dolly Parton."

Dolly knows it is important to know what you don't know and to educate yourself as necessary or partner with people who fill in knowledge gaps. She says, "Learning is all about doing your homework and then taking a chance. The homework part is critical. That means reading (and understanding) feasibility studies, research and hard planning to make sure your ideas make sense. Sometimes it means listening to other experts. It is this studying and thinking through ideas that make projects a true success."

Dolly's first rule of being a professionalist is to be punctual. She always shows up ten minutes early. She feels that if you can't make being on time a priority, you can't necessarily be trusted. Dolly would never show up to an interview or meeting two hours late like many celebrities. She is respectful of her own time and that of others. To her, being on time is keeping a small commitment. If you can't keep a small commitment, how can you be expected to keep the big commitments?

Her second rule is making sure that when she shows up, she is always prepared. When she did her first movie, *9 to 5*, she arrived the first day having memorized the entire script and all the parts, much to the surprise of her costars. Dolly remembered, "It was so funny, 'cause I didn't know exactly what the movies were all about; I just knew that I would do it as good as anybody else. I just assumed they would start in the front and follow the story to keep up the excitement, so I memorized the whole script: my part, Lily's part, Jane's part, every part. But it really worked out great. I got a kick later when I saw how few lines they do a day and how they shoot out of sequence." She knew the script so well she was even feeding lines to her costars when they forgot them.

In *Dream More* she wrote, "Work on a daily basis is about small commitments." Whether you are a boss, an employee, or a coworker, you need to be able to trust that others will do their job and that they, in turn, trust you will do yours. And do it right. Without too much hand-holding. A project or presentation or appearance is a commitment. A deadline is a commitment. An appointment is a commitment. Being consistent builds your reputation and provides some slack and understanding when that once-in-a-lifetime emergency prevents you from fulfilling an obligation. Mutual trust leads to mutual respect. Doing what you say you will over and over again adds up to trust.

Being reliable also applies to your clients, your customers, your boss, your readership, your listeners, or your fans. Dolly shows up on time, looks her best, and gives her fans everything she's got. She knows the importance of her relationship with them. And they are the ones paying the bills! She has said, "If I can't sign autographs, I can always speak and be friendly and say, 'I can't right now. I'm late for a plane.' Because I *do* appreciate it. I think one of the big mistakes celebrities make is that they think because they are so popular, it sets them apart and makes them like gods instead of just extremely lucky people. I really feel sorry for a whole lot of stars, and I hope and pray I never get that way. I don't really believe I will."

No matter how successful she becomes, she still just considers herself a working girl and draws inspiration from her fans. "I enjoy the real people who work all week, who save up money to buy your records and come see you at the show...they're the real thing. It's from them that I draw ideas to write about and create commercial ideas for movies."

It is equally important to be respectful toward your coworkers, your partners, and your employees. Dolly can be tough but as long as you are doing your job and working hard, she is going to treat you extremely well. She says, "I never argue and fight. I'm not temperamental like that." She will give you every chance in the world to succeed, but if you don't, she is going to make some changes. No-nonsense words from the boss herself: "I'm open and I'm honest. I don't dillydally. If there's something going on, I just say it. Sometimes if I get mad, I'll throw out a few cuss words just to prove my point. I've often said I don't lose my temper as much as I use it. I don't do either unless I have to because I love peace and harmony."

That demand that others perform at their highest level goes both ways. Dolly will outwork a mule and, for her, 9 to 5 is an *easy* day. She learned that from her parents and her tough upbringing. The Partons had no choice but to work hard just to survive. She says of her father, "We grew our own food. Daddy would get up in the morning and work till he had to go to his job doing construction. Then he'd come home and still be workin' on the farm till way after dark. We used to soak Daddy's old feet. Mama had some kind of salve she'd made up for Daddy's hands because they'd crack and bleed, and I remember rubbing Daddy's hands with it." It's worth repeating that she not only worked in the fields with her family and went to school but, at age ten, was also waking up before dawn to appear on the Cas Walker show. Before she was a teenager, she was making enough money to support her family, and with that comes a strong sense of responsibility and obligation. They were counting on her and it became a way of life. She loves the work as much as the success.

Kent Wells, a bandleader and coproducer who has worked with Dolly for over twenty-five years, says, "She's inspiring to work with as a businessperson, as a songwriter, as a singer, as a performer. Her work ethic—to be around that is really exciting for me and my team. When she comes in, everybody's in another gear."

Doing just enough to get by is just that, getting by. If you want to succeed and achieve, you need to put in the work. Whatever is required to get it done right. If you're Dolly, that means speaking to almost one hundred reporters in just two days to promote a new album or event. Or working on your show until it is almost perfect. For the rest of us it means burning the midnight oil to get a presentation just right or knocking on just one more door or making one more call to get the sale.

"I've always said I will step over you or around you to get where I'm going but I will never step on you."

"I Will Always Love You"

Dolly wrote her most successful song at the end of her time on Porter Wagoner's show in an effort to get him to let her leave to pursue a solo career. It was 1973 and after seven years together he wouldn't let her go. She went home and wrote the song, which she says was a message to Porter that leaving his show didn't mean she wouldn't always appreciate him and love him. The next day she brought it in and sang it to Porter, who got tears in his eyes. He said it was the prettiest song he had ever heard and that he would let her go if she allowed him to produce it, which he did. She sang and recorded it and it debuted at number one on the Hot Country Songs chart.

Not long after, Elvis wanted to record the song and Dolly was ecstatic, running around telling everyone, and she was invited down to the studio to watch him. The night before the recording, Colonel Tom, Elvis's notoriously tough manager, called her and said, "You know, Elvis doesn't record anything that he doesn't have the publishing rights to, so he'll need fifty percent." As much as it killed her to do it, she said no, because she felt that it was the most important song in her publishing catalog. Remember at the time that Elvis was a major superstar and Dolly was just a girl singer starting out on her solo career, so that took some guts. Elvis didn't record the song, which just about broke her heart, but she kept the publishing rights, which paid off in the end.

Years later when Whitney Houston recorded the song for the movie *The Bodyguard*, Dolly got a windfall to the tune of millions of dollars. Maureen Crowe, the musical supervisor of the film, says that Kevin Costner originally wanted "What Becomes of the Broken Hearted" by Jimmy Ruffin, but Paul Young ended up recording it for the film *Fried Green Tomatoes* and it was climbing the charts. Kevin still wanted to use it but Maureen told him he would look like a copycat if he did. (It is also a pretty depressing song when it is slowed down to a ballad speed.) So Maureen got a copy of the Linda Ronstadt version of "I Will Always Love You" and Kevin said okay, but he wanted a male voice singing it and he didn't want it to sound too country. Eventually he brought the song to Whitney, and music producer David Foster repurposed it as a pop song for her. They recorded it live at the Fontainebleau in Miami in March 1992 and Whitney blew it into the stratosphere. The song came out before the movie did and reached number one and became a huge part of the successful marketing of the movie. It spent fourteen weeks at number one and became one of the best-selling singles of all time. It's also the first song to debut at number one three times—over forty-two years.

The first time Dolly heard Whitney's version, she was in the car listening to the radio. "All of a sudden I hear this… this a capella sound, I just hear this, 'If I should stay,' and it didn't register, and I thought, 'What is that?'" Parton said, and then, "'That's my song,' but it still didn't register it was Whitney, because it was just this solo voice, and then all of a sudden it went into the 'I will always love you,' and I thought I was gonna wreck. It just overwhelmed me."

It became the anthem of Whitney's career. When they played it at her funeral, it just crushed Dolly because her premature death was so painful for her to deal with, especially given their history with this song.

Stiletto Through the Glass Ceiling

Work hard at staying relevant in a world that is constantly changing. Dolly has noticed that other careers in music have not proved as lasting as her own, "and people are bitter about it. But you'll find they stopped." What does she mean by that? She means that they have stopped caring, stopped learning and evolving, stopped being creative, or stopped going out on the road and doing the day-to-day hard work of promoting a record and giving back to your audience. Dolly is constantly moving on to the next thing and learning new things and as a result her professional portfolio runs deep and wide.

When she left *The Porter Wagoner Show* in 1974 to pursue a solo career, she hired Hollywood super-manager Sandy Gallin to help her cross over into the mainstream and to start a film career. She received a ton of criticism and faced a lot of skepticism. The country music world in Nashville was resentful that she was leaving them and wanted her to fail. They thought she had "gone Hollywood." Tex Lively, a DJ at KPIK in Colorado Springs, said he wouldn't play her on the radio anymore and was quoted as saying, "all of us feel like she deserted the country folks." The country folks, in turn, deserted her.

Despite the criticism, which surely hurt her, she pushed on and reinvented herself as a film actress and pop artist and as a result gained more creative and financial freedom. Any time you make a move or set your ambitions high, you are going to make some people uncomfortable. Ignore them. Don't take their criticism personally and just keep moving forward with your plans.

Her biggest hit up until that point was "Jolene," which despite being a number one country hit sold only 60,000 copies. She knew if she could cross over, she could sell closer to a million copies—or more—of a record. It was simple economics and she needed to make more money after paying Porter in order to get off his show. He took all of her money in the settlement and put her underwater financially for several years. She had the confidence and talent, and together with her team came up with a strategy to get out from under and grow. It worked.

Many years later she complained that she couldn't get a record played on the radio because she was considered "old country." At the time she bemoaned, "The music business is not what it used to be. After you reach a certain age, they think you're over. Well, I will never be over. I'll be making records if I have to sell them out of the trunk of my car. I've done that in the past, and I'd do it again." The music industry isn't the only one that has this kind of ageism. The only way to deal with it is to keep momentum going and keep trying new things to stay relevant.

If success is what you want, you have to be willing to step out of your comfort zone. When Jane Fonda was pulling together *9 to 5*, she wanted Dolly Parton. She had never met her but was a big fan of her music and created the character of Doralee around Dolly's persona and just let her go with it. Despite having never acted before or as much as taken an acting lesson, Dolly dove in feetfirst, killed it in the role, and launched her successful career in Hollywood, not only as an actress but eventually also as a successful producer. Jane later said, "This was not a woman who was a stereotype of a dumb blonde. I felt that she could probably do just about anything she wanted, that this was a very smart woman."

In her "middle years," she went without management for almost seventeen years and hadn't been doing a whole lot that was putting her at the forefront of her industry. Being inducted into the Country Music Hall of Fame in 1999 could have been considered the culmination of her goals, and financially she didn't need to make any more money. In the early 2000s, she met Danny Nozell, a hotshot manager who decided he was going to put her back on the map and find her a whole new audience with younger people, and together they found it. Being so popular and relevant in recent years was no accident; it was a strategy. They worked together to take Dolly's lists and goals, which, as we know, are all written down, and use them to develop a concrete five-year plan. Once that plan has been accomplished, she moves on to the next five-year plan.

She reached that whole new audience in a big way after playing the Glastonbury music festival in 2014. They had asked her to play every year from 2006 until 2013, and she was afraid to do it, thinking she wouldn't appeal to that crowd. She finally took the leap and when she got onstage she faced the largest audience to show up for a performer in Glastonbury's history. One hundred eighty thousand fans let out a roar of approval, many of them dressed up like her, and they all sang along to her hits. In 2007 and beyond, her tours to Europe and Australia sold out, and her 2016 North American tour was the largest and most successful of her career.

Dolly's explanation for her youth appeal is, "I think people think of me more as an aunt or sister because they've grown up with me. The reason I think I have a lot of young people [is] because a lot of older ones have played my records. With the little kids, [it's] my Imagination Library, where I give books out to children and that I was Hannah Montana's aunt on that very hip show, so that gave me a new audience. I just always manage to be on the job. I didn't want them to forget me, so I try to stay out front."

In 2017 she sang a duet of her 1980 hit "Old Flames Can't Hold a Candle to You" on Kesha's first album in several years, *Rainbow* (how apropos!). Dolly knows Kesha's mother, Pebe Sebert, who is a songwriter in Nashville who originally cowrote "Old Flames" and was delighted when Kesha called her to collaborate.

And she came out with her very first children's album, *I Believe in You*, at age seventy-one. She wrote all of the tracks on the album based on her own experiences, and they are meant to give children confidence, to be brave, to be kind, and to not be bullies. She has really come full circle and still has so much more she wants to do, including a movie of her own life story.

We can't wait to see what the next five-year plan holds.

9 to 5

One day Jane Fonda was driving and a song of Dolly's came on the radio. The proverbial lightbulb went off in Jane's head—Dolly would be the right combination with her and Lily Tomlin and she would help get the Southern demographics into the theaters. Meanwhile, Dolly wanted to break into the movies and was reading, and turning down, a lot of scripts and offers. She wanted to find the right fit at the right time.

Dolly was excited that they wanted her and she accepted because she loved the script, and she knew that having Jane and Lily as main characters as well took some of the pressure off her. She said that if she were to do a movie on her own and it flopped, it would have been Dolly Parton's flop, but having Jane and Lily there, too, meant if it flopped she could place some of the blame on them! She said, "A lot of people were sayin', 'Boy, I would *l-o-o-o-v-e* to see that. There ain't no way them three bitches are gonna get along! Can you imagine three women like that?!' And you know, we had the greatest time."

It was a great career move for Dolly and allowed people to see her terrific sense of humor. She also wrote half of the songs on the soundtrack, including, of course, the iconic theme song "9 to 5," which became one of her biggest hits. She used her daddy, her family, and her friends as inspiration as the working people who deal with the grind day after day.

Don't Be Hick Rich

In her 1977 Barbara Walters interview, Dolly explained to the general public why she had found new management in an effort to move into pop music and Hollywood: "I have worked too hard for too long for too little. Why make thousands when I can make millions?" Right on, sister! Up until that point, even though she was touring a lot and considered successful, her top-grossing record was "Jolene," which made her only around $200,000 in royalties. She knew she could do better than that and made the effort to invest in expanding her career and making more money.

As we mentioned, Dolly's net worth is in the ballpark of $650 million, which may be a conservative estimate, and it is something she built over time in a deliberate way. And while she owns several houses, she considers those investments. Much of her money goes into investing into new business ventures and she lets her success build on success. Part of her investment strategy is to never put all of her eggs in one basket, or diversify as soon as she is able. She spent $1 million in 2007 to launch her own record label, Dolly Records, as an investment in herself at a time when the music industry wasn't supporting her, thinking that, because she was of a certain age she was "over." She recouped her investment with her next album in three months.

· Some people who make money quick spend it quicker. Don't do that. After growing up so poor, Dolly wanted all of the nice things she never had, but she also knows the value of a dollar. She isn't frivolous or wasteful. And so much of the money she makes is invested back into her businesses or given to her family or into her philanthropy. She says that she will "never spend a lot of money on something without thinking about it. That don't mean you don't spend the money. But you do it with thought. I'm glad that I can spend now and have the things that I want and need. If I wanted something, I would go and get it, but usually I like for other people to have nice things, like my family."

She witnessed firsthand when her generation in the music business wasn't being played on the radio anymore and was being replaced by the younger, up-and-coming talent. She didn't struggle financially during those times because she had other things going on. But she did watch many of her friends in the business struggle. They spent their money as soon as they made it. That's hick rich.

There's a fine line between being hick rich and investing in yourself. It's helpful to know the difference. One is frivolous and the other strategic. One of the first things Dolly bought as soon as she had a regular paycheck was a Cadillac, which she saw as a symbol of success, and she knew others in the business would see it as such, too. At first glance it might look like a hick rich thing to do—and it probably is in a lot of cases—but Dolly felt that driving a brand-new Cadillac around town made a statement to other people; it showed them she was doing well and put her in demand. In a way you could argue that buying that car was an investment in her continued success. It's like making sure you show up at a job interview well dressed with a nice pair of shoes. Dressing for success is an investment in your career. Spending a fortune on designer shoes you can't afford just because you think they're pretty is being hick rich.

Dolly's father told her to never trust someone else with your money and she has heeded his advice. In other words, don't just hand your money over to an "expert" or investor and think that they know more than you. That doesn't mean you don't get sound financial advice when making investment decisions. Just don't be ignorant about where your money is; educate yourself on basic personal finance, or business finance as needed, and brush up on your financial education as necessary. Know where your money is and keep an eye on it so you can ask the right questions or make the right decisions as need be.

Just Because I'm a Woman: Dolly as Feminist Icon

Just listen to the lyrics from her admonishment of sexual double standards in 1968's "Just Because I'm a Woman" or her working girl anthem "9 to 5," and it is clear that despite her proclaiming time and again, "I have never been a feminist," Dolly may not talk the talk but she sure does walk the walk. Many of the earliest songs she wrote and built her career on were pretty direct about confronting double standards. Just listen to "Your Ole Handyman," "He's A Go Getter," "When Possession Gets Too Strong," and "Daddy."

In 1987, Gloria Steinem wrote an article about Dolly for *Ms.* magazine, stating that she "has turned all the devalued symbols of womanliness to her own ends." She has long been accused of exploiting her own femininity. Well, yeah! Better that she owns it than let someone else exploit her.

Her take on it is, "I grew up around lots of men so I wasn't intimidated by them and feeling pretty and sexy actually empowered me." In other words, she's got this.

Dolly, in an effort to avoid controversy, turned to making jokes about it, regularly telling "boob" jokes and saying, "I was the first woman to burn my bra—it took the fire department four days to put it out." When *Billboard* magazine asked her in 2014 if she had heard of Sheryl Sandberg's book *Lean In*, she said she didn't know it and that she had "leaned over. I've leaned forward. I don't know what 'leaned in' is."

And yet she doesn't mince words when talking about the challenges that women face. She said:

> Being a woman in show-business is like being a bird dog in heat. If you stand still they'll screw you. If you run they'll bite you in the ass...A smart woman can take a man who thinks with his small head and quickly turn the would-be screwer into the screwee...I never slept with anybody to get ahead in my career. It didn't take long for them to realize I wasn't there to sell my body, but because my work was worthy. I'd say, "I have a gift and think I can make us both a lot of money— are you interested?" and they usually were.

Regardless of the feminist label and how it is interpreted, Dolly is no doubt a strong role model for women. The evidence speaks for itself. She is self-made and created her own financial independence. She owns all of her businesses and manages them, hiring people whom she trusts and overseeing all of it. She broke through the patriarchal Nashville music establishment, refusing to just be a "girl singer." When it was clear that *The Porter Wagoner Show* was becoming the Dolly Parton show, she fought hard to leave and start her own solo career. She also does marriage her own way and works under her own name. She saw so many of her peers' careers fizzle out once they became wives and mothers and made it clear from the beginning of her marriage that her career was a priority and that her husband and her business would not be mingled.

WWDD TO CREATE AND MAINTAIN A SUCCESSFUL CAREER?

- Be a professionalist: be punctual, be prepared, keep your commitments.
- Respect your coworkers, partners, employees, and audience.
- 9 to 5 is an easy day—have a strong work ethic.
- Be the Queen of Reinvention to stay relevant.
- Have a five-year plan.
- Diversify your career and your investments.
- Invest in yourself.

Chapter Seven

Find Your Angels

Have the Right People in Your Life

*D*olly has almost a sixth sense when it comes to knowing whom she can trust. She feels she has been blessed with great people in her life, but she also attracts them and has a strong bullshit detector that she says she got from her daddy. He "could look at a person across the yard and tell if they were honest and sincere or a crook. I'm like that too." She has incredible, supportive people in her life, but when you are as high-profile as she is, it is inevitable that people will try to take advantage of or betray you, no matter how people-savvy you may be. She has been swift in eliminating the guilty or being incredibly forgiving. As a result, she has learned not to deal with creative or emotional vampires.

Jane Fonda has said, "Dolly is, in my opinion, canny about life and people." Finding the right people to have in your life, eliminating the bad ones, and making an effort to spread kindness and bring joy are all conscious efforts Dolly makes in relating to other people.

She knows that relationships can make or break you and are the foundation for a happy life. She also strongly believes that when you make it, you have a responsibility to lift up everyone else around you. Her combination of street smarts and generosity of spirit have served her well. She knows that it's not enough to have dreams and work hard. "You gotta have people to help carry out those dreams, and, Lord, I've been surrounded by great people."

Many of her relationships have lasted since childhood or her early career. She still keeps her siblings and family members close and many of them work for her. She is closely involved with the many people who work for her or with her and has maintained relationships over several decades.

The two most important people in her life, her rocks, have been her best friend since childhood and her husband of more than fifty years. She calls Judy and Carl "the two greatest gifts God ever gave me. I can't imagine what my life would have been without them." Indeed, having such a loyal, lifetime best friend and a solid, loving, and accepting husband is more than most of us get. They both knew her before she became a star and their love and support have been invaluable to her. She met Judy around the time they were seven years old, and in the movie *Coat of Many Colors* Judy is portrayed as the quiet "ghostlike" moonshiner's daughter. She is the one who comes to Dolly's rescue when the other kids are making fun of her, tearing at her coat and locking her in the closet. Young Dolly says to her in thanks, "That's angel work," and Judy replies, "Friends fight for each other; that's what they do."

"Over the years I have had a few angels in my life . . . these angels have helped me succeed, taught me things I needed to understand to grow, and returned my love."

Take Care of Your Own

Despite her incredible success, Dolly has managed to do something so many stars don't—maintain her down-to-earth nature. She never forgot where she came from, saying, "I mean we were really Hill Billies. To me that's not an insult. We were just mountain people. We were really redneck, roughneck, hillbilly people. And I'm proud of it...To me that keeps you humble; that keeps you good. And it doesn't matter how hard you try to outrun it—if that's who you are, that's who you are. It'll show up once in a while."

Time after time, people report on how down-to-earth she is, which comes from the values she grew up with. Taking care of your own means taking care of the other people around you, sometimes just by having good manners. The writer for the Broadway musical *9 to 5*, Patricia Resnick, remembers a lunch at her home with Dolly and the producer of the play, Robert Greenblatt. After lunch, Dolly, like the good country girl she is, brought her dish to the sink and rinsed it off, which stunned them. Despite being wildly famous, Dolly tries not to act like she is better than anyone else or let her stardom make her think she is somehow above the simple things, like common courtesy or being a good guest.

In interview after interview, journalists all seem to comment on how darn nice Dolly is. She seems to genuinely enjoy people and making them happy. When Bryan Miller at the *New York Times* took her to lunch for an interview to promote her movie *Straight Talk*, he noted that she gets along just as well with cabbies and waiters as she does with Hollywood moguls.

Dolly has that gift of making other people feel like they're someone special. She looks them in the eye; she gives them her time; she listens. And no matter how famous she has become, she remains accessible and sincere.

She is proud of her roots and she doesn't stray too far from them. It was always important for her to go back home and do something that would make her family and her people proud.

There's an old saying, "We take care of our own," and Dolly and her people, and the country folk she grew up around, all live by this saying. This is more than Dolly taking care of her family by buying them a house or a car or taking in her younger siblings once she became successful. Her family beyond her parents, siblings, nephews and nieces, aunts and uncles, and in-laws includes hundreds of people from the area and they all take care of one another in good times and bad. Big sister Willadeene writes in her family memoir, "We have...a side that grieves when neighbors have hard times, a side that is strong in the face of trouble, and a side that helps people in need. When the aid is given, whether it is gathering crops for a man who's sick, taking food to a family that has none, or helping rebuild a house that has burned, it's done with the words, 'Don't thank me. I might need help someday, and you'd do the same for me.'" This philosophy explains why Dolly has given so much back to her community and why she shares so much with her family. Mountain people consider it shameful for one member or part of the family to be well off while another is struggling and poor. As a result, she has helped not just her hometown but has also almost single-handedly helped improve the economy and well-being of her entire region.

The women around her served as strong role models in this regard. She may have starred in a movie called *Steel Magnolias* but that phrase existed long before Truvy opened her beauty parlor in the fictional movie town Chinquapin, Louisiana. A steel magnolia is a strong, resilient, but still very feminine Southern woman. Growing up, Dolly saw the women in her family as the heroes who kept things going. Avie Lee had to do so for family time and time again, whether it was the heroic act of feeding and clothing twelve children on a daily basis or keeping the family alive when they were trapped in the house for several days during a blizzard.

Dolly grew up with strong Southern women all around her. She says that her mother; grandmothers; and aunts, especially Dorothy Jo Owens, who was a preacher and songwriter, showed her how to be strong. It was the women who maintained the family during tough times and when the men ran off on a bender or to go work a town or a state away because it was the only work available. Dolly told *Southern Living*, "The women kept the families going. So I really am just proud to be a good ol' Southern gal. And I really am in my spirit and in my heart. Because I see so much of my family in the things that I do. And I love and embrace that."

With twelve children and minimal to no health care, her mama was sick much of the time and so the older children would care for the younger children. Avie Lee's sister Estelle Watson says, "Avie Lee always had imagination. I guess that's where Dolly gets that. Avie's a great mother and a fine person." Avie Lee's strong faith was the foundation of the family.

Avie Lee also sang old folk songs and Elizabethan ballads and told great stories from the Bible, as well as ghost stories and tall tales. They did family sing-alongs, and seven out of the twelve Parton children work as musicians. Even though Dolly and her siblings didn't have TV or toys growing up, they had their mama, who not only stretched the food enough to feed them all but also made them toys out of household items, hammered a spool on the screen door as a doorknob, and lovingly sewed their clothes. She also supported the dreams of each and every one of them. The Parton children grew up totally free to express themselves. Avie Lee didn't criticize their aspirations or destroy their belief in their talents.

Once Dolly became successful, she showed her appreciation by trying to buy Avie Lee a mink coat. Avie Lee asked her where on earth she would wear a mink coat—to a church supper? So Dolly gave her the money instead. She eventually bought her mama her first car and several brightly colored pantsuits, telling her that she was giving her freedom. It was the first time her mother learned to drive or wore pants, and Avie Lee spent so much time driving around in her new clothes that Papa complained she was neglecting him. Dolly also bought her parents a new house and had it fully renovated and decorated, down to the smallest detail. When Avie Lee passed away, her estate was worth more than 1 million dollars.

Despite the love the Parton family shared, they didn't say it out loud very often. One day after Dolly had not lived at home for a while, she was saying goodbye to her father and when she told him "I love you," he looked at the ground and didn't say anything back, which was typical of him. She took his face in her hands and made him say it and finally he stuttered and stammered but he did it. And from then on the whole family started saying it to each other freely.

She says Carl doesn't really say it much either. When he asked her to marry him, she responded by saying that he had never even told her that he loved her. His answer was, "Hell, you know I love you." Dolly likes to hear it and has had to train her husband and family members accordingly.

Dolly believes it's important to show up for the people close to you and to communicate your love and appreciation. It may take some training—of them or you—but it's an important thing to share. There's no reason to take people for granted or regret, after it's too late, not telling them how you feel. Love, and our relationships, are what sustain us and lift us up.

You Can't Make Old Friends

Dolly depends on her best friend, Judy Ogle, for a lot of things. "Y'know, you often hear that stars who died sadly, like Elvis and Marilyn Monroe, had all kinds of people around them, but you never hear that they had a best friend, someone who really knew them and loved them. Well, I have Judy." Judy works as her personal assistant but is so much more than that. She takes care of her; she is sometimes the one who writes down the lyrics to songs as Dolly comes up with them; she makes sure everything is running smoothly; and she also is a confidante, a companion, and, more than anything, a good friend. "We're absolutely, totally honest with each other. We've been accused of being lovers. We do love each other but we've never been like that."

The false rumors have dogged Dolly for years, especially since Carl is so rarely seen in public or the press, and Judy, as her right-hand person, travels with her on the road. She has often said that she is closer to Judy than to Carl and doesn't see why anyone would think there's anything wrong with that. She also doesn't see what would be wrong if the rumors were true. Dolly has many, many gay friends, which is to be expected in the entertainment business, and she can't understand why this is a big deal or why anyone cares about her sexuality. She has said that there are a lot of gay people in the world and she loves them but she's just not one of them.

She compares her relationship with Judy to Oprah's

relationship with Gayle King, saying people "just think that you just can't be that close to somebody. Judy and I have been best friends since we were like in the third and fourth grade...We still just have a great friendship and relationship and I love her as much as I love anybody in the whole world, but we're not romantically involved."

Judy also gets along well with Carl, which is a big plus. Dolly says, "Carl and Judy are very good friends and they are there for each other...She comes over to pick me up and if she has a low tire, he will check her car and raise the hood and look at it and say, 'We need to look at this fan belt.' No matter what we're going through personally or business wise, they're there for me as I am for them."

One of her oldest friends is Kenny Rogers, who said that when the two of them made "Islands in the Stream," they connected musically, but when they made "You Can't Make Old Friends," they connected personally. That song is really about them and their thirty-year relationship. Despite years of rumors, they have both confirmed that they have a close, loving relationship but it is nothing romantic or sexual. To her, a friend is a friend, whether male or female.

Those relationships that you've had for a long time are not easily replicated. She has known Judy since they were seven, Carl since she was eighteen, and has had many other long-time friends over the years. As much as she loves people and getting to know them and making new friends, she is right when she says that you can't make old friends. They are the ones who knew you when, who will keep you grounded and remind you of who you are when the world gets out of hand. They are the ones who you know love you for the true you, no matter how rich or famous you become.

A Girl's Got to Get Away

The girls of the Parton family, Dolly and her five sisters—Stella, Cassie, Freida, Rachel, and Willadeene—plan annual "girls only" vacations. Each year a different family member is in charge of the theme and planning and brings everyone to their chosen location as a surprise. They are so secret that not even their husbands or children know where they are going or what they will do while they are there. In her book *Smoky Mountain Memories*, Dolly's oldest sister, Willadeene, shared her diary of the time when Avie Lee was in charge of planning and brought her fully grown daughters to the old cabin they grew up in. She had fully decorated it to look exactly like their childhood home, made an old country–style supper, and filled trunks with old love letters that boys had written to them. They stayed up all night telling stories and singing songs. Celebrating your shared history keeps you grounded and provides emotional support and perspective through life's ups and downs.

Dolly and Judy also go on a lot of girl trips, and the two of them will jump into an RV with no wig or makeup and travel in total privacy. They will go on long drives in the camper, spend time on retreat at one of Dolly's homes in California, or go and write songs at her old Tennessee Mountain home for a couple of weeks. These trips are crucial to her spiritual and mental well-being because she knows that Judy knows her better than anyone and will listen to whatever it is she has to say without judgment. These are the times when Dolly can regroup, talk things through, and get moral support and advice.

Have Good Old-Fashioned Horse Sense

Dolly's ability to judge a person's character has served her well. Sometimes that good old-fashioned horse sense just means following her gut when it comes to having people come into her life. She says she always prays for God to put the right people in her life and take all the wrong people out.

Committing to the right people and creating true partnerships is the difference between success and failure, professionally and personally. It is a two-way street built on trust, which is created through consistency, dependency, and mutual commitment.

Dolly is the first person to acknowledge the many strong mentors in her life. Her uncle Bill Owens was the first one to really believe in her talent. Not only did he replace her homemade two-stringed mandolin with a real baby Martin guitar, but they also eventually became songwriting partners. He encouraged her when she was young, set her up with her first radio appearance, and took her to Nashville, showing her the ropes and introducing her to the music business. With his help getting her a regular slot singing for Cas Walker's show, she was earning more in two years than her father ever could. He also arranged her first studio recording when she was just thirteen for her single "Puppy Love," which they cowrote. She rode a bus for the first time, with her grandmother, all the way to Lake Charles, Louisiana, to make the record.

You could say Uncle Bill was her first manager. When she moved to Nashville, she stayed with Uncle Bill and his wife and babysat their child in exchange for room and board in a trailer alongside their house. Dolly says that "everything, or at least a lot of things, that I did in the early part of my career he was responsible for."

Fred Foster at Monument Records was the first person to take a chance on her in Nashville. The other music execs thought her voice was too high and shrill. One even said she sounded like a screech owl. When she dropped her demo off at Monument, Fred liked what he heard. His peers had warned him, and Dolly even warned him, that everyone else had turned her down. But he liked her and thought she had everything she needed to succeed and signed her. She says she was really unpolished and naïve at that point but that he saw "a diamond in the rough." He backed her first breakout hit recording, ironically a song she didn't write, "Dumb Blonde" by Curly Putman. Fred wanted a hit song for her and introduced her to Curly, who said, "Well you are no dumb blonde," and from there wrote the song just for her.

During her seven years on Porter Wagoner's show, she learned a tremendous amount from him. He taught her stage presence, showmanship, and how to connect with an audience. He was a flashy dresser with colorful, sequined wagon-wheel suits, which encouraged her to create her own flashier image and costumes. He produced her records, got her a contract with RCA, and taught her the ins and outs of the music business. The two of them had great chemistry on the air and would flirt and banter so much that the rumors flew about them being romantically involved. Dolly says she will always be grateful to him for all that he taught her and for how hard he worked to help build her career. But more on that in a minute.

Jane Fonda and Lily Tomlin mentored her through her first film, *9 to 5*, and the three of them became good friends and had a great time working together. Jane created a character for her that allowed Dolly to shine and to basically be herself, since she had never acted before or had a lesson. And it turned Dolly into a household name.

Partnering with the right people is important, and having a good partner can be the difference between being successful or not. Especially when you are venturing into new areas or industries where you are not an expert.

Some of the best business decisions you can make are about surrounding yourself with top-notch people who share your vision. Any good boss knows that you have to give credit where credit is due. Dolly knows this well and tells interviewers, "I get a lot of credit for a lot of work that a lot of other people do." But she is certainly in there overseeing and managing everything.

When Dolly was ready to try breaking into the mainstream, she hired Sandy Gallin as her new manager. Sandy was managing Cher and Joan Rivers at the time and Mac Davis, who toured with Dolly. When she told Mac that she wanted to broaden her audience, he recommended she call Sandy. Despite being as different as they possibly could be, they ended up becoming great friends and business partners for twenty-five years. When they first met she got all dressed up for him in an all-white, sparkly getup trying to impress him. When he came to pick her up he looked very elegant, driving a Mercedes convertible and wearing corduroys and penny loafers. He took one look at her and burst out laughing. He then took her to his mansion, where his personal chefs cooked them a meal and he let her borrow some more conservative clothes. She said that he was "as L.A. as a person could get and me twice as Nashville as the neon sign at Twitty City." But they shared the determination to make her succeed along with their high-energy personalities and deep spiritual lives. They were something like soul mates. She says he was the only person, other than her uncle Bill Owens, who wanted her to be a success more than she did. He knew if she could get a good pop hit out, she would cross over. He convinced her to record "Here You Come Again," which went to number one on the Hot Country Songs chart, number three on the pop charts, won her a Grammy for best female country vocalist, and went platinum.

In 1985, they started a film and television production company together, Sandollar, which amassed numerous awards, including an Academy Award for the documentary *Common Threads: Stories from the Quilt.*

Given Carl's homebody nature and lack of desire to travel around or live for periods of time in New York, he was happy that Sandy took such good care of her. Sandy was more than just a business partner and friend, and Dolly called him the "earth angel" who picked her up and helped put her back together after her depression, weight gain, health problems, and career hiatus. She said, "He came to my rescue like a knight in corduroy armor." He took her to New York to meet with different doctors when she was sick, and they even shared a Fifth Avenue penthouse apartment in New York for several years. He tried to expose her to "culture" and furnished the living room with expensive art and books for her to read. She said he also decorated the place: "That's when Sandy here comes in handy. He's got taste and I got talent."

Every girl should be lucky enough to have a gay best friend or two, for companionship, sharing, and doing things together that regular husbands may not be interested in, whether it's traveling, going out and dancing in nightclubs, shopping, or going to the theater. Sandy traveled around the world with her and the two of them spent time at Studio 54, a place where Carl wouldn't be caught dead.

When she opened Dollywood and her other resorts, she hired the local people to keep it real but found industry experts to help her run those companies. She teamed up with Herschend Family Entertainment, which owned several amusement and theme parks, including Silver Dollar City in her hometown of Pigeon Forge. They turned Silver Dollar City into Dollywood and started dinner theaters in the area. Herschend eventually created a separate division called the Dollywood Company specifically to oversee all of Dolly's interests.

She started the Dollywood Foundation and hired people who knew how to make philanthropy effective. She interviewed David Dotson, who has been the president of the Dollywood Foundation for many years, in the back of a van, and after talking for about ten minutes she decided she liked him and hired him. He understood philanthropy, and under him, the foundation—and especially the Imagination Library—have grown and expanded all over the world.

With Dolly's diverse business interests, her list of partners is long and varied. Some are relatively new partners and some have been around for most of her career. After Sandy Gallin left the entertainment business to begin a home design business, Dolly didn't have management for fourteen years. When she was preparing to go on tour, she needed someone to help her organize her tour and was led to Danny Nozell. He became her new manager, helping her reevaluate and revive her career. Throughout the decades she always had Don Warden, whom she originally met when he was working on Porter's show. When she left the show, Don went with her and worked for her until he passed away in 2016. She called him her "Mr. Everything" and "#1 Angel" because he handled so many of the day-to-day details of her shows and merchandising, in addition to being a mentor who knew all the different aspects of the music business. His wife, Ann, decorated many of her properties and he was even her bus driver, traveling with her for years.

Turn Your Devils into Angels

Dolly has much better things to do than deal with negative people or toxic relationships. There will always be people in your life who take away more energy than they give. Unfortunately, not everyone has your best interests at heart. They may be jealous. They may want to feel better about themselves by undermining you. They may always be asking you for help but don't reciprocate. They may just want to blame you for their problems or incompetence. Dolly says that the sooner you realize these people are vampires, the sooner you can deal with them and get on with your life, whether they are family members, friends, or business associates.

She has been blackmailed by people that she knew and had a family member she calls "the Squealer," who was selling false stories to the tabloids and built quite the successful business doing so. The Squealer turned out to be an aunt who had moved away when Dolly was very young, so they barely knew each other. She was selling stories to the tabloids and trying to appear on TV talk shows to diss Dolly over some old, imagined slight. Dolly doesn't elaborate on how she dealt with her, but says she took care of it, but not as harshly as she could have. Given Dolly's nature, we can imagine that she confronted her and just told her to stop. That was probably enough without having to go into threats or lawsuits, which would just waste more time and energy.

During tough times or at certain life milestones, it's a good idea to pause and take inventory of the people around you and clean house. On Dolly's fortieth birthday, after her painful recovery from surgery, depression, and betrayal by some of the people closest to her, she did just that. She wrote letters to four people who were part of her family and her business, who she felt had had the upper hand on her for many years. "The letters were very blunt. They said, I'm not going to put up with your B.S. anymore. You have no control over me and little control over yourself, so you should examine things very carefully. Then I made some phone calls too. I decided to get all the grief and worries over irresponsible people out of my life. And it worked—it really cleared the air. I'm perfectly comfortable with those people now."

When your relationships are no longer emotionally beneficial or they bring out the worst in you, or others, you need to make some painful decisions. And when things get tough, don't just place blame but take a good look in the mirror. Sometimes the most challenging relationships can also be the biggest learning experiences. This isn't easy for anyone, especially when these people are family or have been close to you for years.

She says of herself, "I have a tendency to be awfully big hearted and it's very hard for me to say no, even when I need to. I can handle the business—the bigger they are the better I like dealing with them—but when it gets into business where I'm very attached to the people, it's hard."

There are also times when she had to fire people close to her and endure periods of stress with her parents and siblings. She told Andy Warhol how difficult it was to go back and address long-lingering family issues and the realities of dealing with them: "At the time I was making some decisions, making myself go way, way back to muddy waters. When you spend your whole life working...I had to make some decisions that I needed to make for years, but I kept holding on because I loved these people so much." Being direct and loving in handling difficult relationships and situations can make the relationship even stronger.

Dolly's forgiving and compassionate nature allows her to take the long view when dealing with people. She also knows that sometimes God puts difficult people in front of you as teachers.

She has called the seven years she worked with Porter the hardest and worst period of her life but also the most productive and growth filled. She felt stifled by him and was writing a lot of their songs without getting credit. As the producer, he made final creative calls that often left her frustrated. Their "knock-down, drag-outs" became the stuff of legend.

When she finally left to go on her own, Porter was bitter and their relationship took an even worse turn, which evolved into a lawsuit, bad blood, and a lot of tit for tat in the press. He felt he had "created" her and therefore was owed compensation and sued her in a complicated legal battle in which she had to give him a significant amount of money that, at the time, she didn't really have. She had to sell a lot of her assets to pay him off, which caused her financial hardship for several years. But she paid him and even though it was a bitter pill to swallow, she saw it as a point of pride and perhaps as a way of buying her freedom. It most likely drove her even harder to succeed on her own.

The depth of Dolly's forgiving nature was revealed when years later they appeared onstage together and she sang "I Will Always Love You" to him, and she was one of the people at his bedside when he was dying. She chose to learn from the whole relationship and experience and rise above it.

And it didn't hurt that "I Will Always Love You" made her millions and millions of dollars over four decades.

Dolly is a good and forgiving soul and, by all accounts, treats the people around her with generosity and has maintained her accessible nature. Her philosophy is, "It's important to me that I accomplish things as a human being, as it should be to all people to accomplish all that they can without sacrificing other people. I didn't sacrifice the happiness of other people to get where I am."

WWDD IN HER RELATIONSHIPS WITH OTHERS?

- Never forget where you come from.
- Stick with people you trust in business and life.
- Tell people you love and appreciate them; give credit where credit is due.
- Find the right mentors.
- Then find the right partners.
- Avoid negative people and creative vampires.
- Sometimes you have to clean house, but do it kindly and directly.
- Don't sacrifice the happiness of others to get where you want to go.

Chapter Eight

Tennessee Mountain Home

$\mathcal{Y}$ou can take the girl out of the country but you can't take the country out of the girl. Although Dolly's childhood home was simple by any standards, it had a powerful impact on shaping her idea of what home is. Two hundred fifteen miles west of Nashville, the two-room wood cabin had a tin roof that sometimes leaked and an inelegant front porch. It sat on Locust Ridge Road in Pigeon Forge at the end of a gravel road surrounded by fields and small pieces of farmland. Despite its lack of modern amenities, such as electricity or running water, Dolly felt loved and secure within her large family. She also loved growing up so close to nature. Her memories of that home continue to inspire her music and her favorite recreational activities, and make her feel grounded.

For Dolly, home is about resting, relaxing, and recharging. She likes to be with Carl, her siblings and nieces and nephews, enjoying the simple pleasures like cooking and reading or doing country things, like taking walks in the woods, going on picnics, or sitting outside on the porch talking. Leaving her professional life behind when she is home is how she maintains her sanity. She lets her hair down—which means taking her wig off—goes without makeup, and walks around half-nekkid if she wants to without the outside world imposing on her.

Home is a place to nourish your soul and replenish your heart. For Dolly that place is Willow Lake in Brentwood, Tennessee, the only home that Carl and Dolly call "the home place." Carl spends most of his time there and it's where Dolly goes when she "goes home." She says that she and Carl are "pretty much old mountain goats."

Everyone has a right to their downtime and privacy, and Dolly is no exception. Willow Lake is set back far and on a road small enough that tour buses can't get there. The privacy allows Carl to do his work in peace. The two of them can sit on the front porch and just enjoy each other's company without the rest of the world's intrusions.

When Dolly is in the public eye, no matter where she goes, she is perfectly put together in wig, glamorous clothes, and full makeup. She even shows up for photo shoots at 5:00 a.m. in full Dolly regalia. The last thing she wants to do is disappoint her fans. Dolly's philosophy is, "I don't believe we owe everything to the public. I think I have a right to my privacy, and I also feel that people have a right to the time I'm in public. That is *their* time." Being home provides her with a respite where she can maintain her balance. "Now, there is nothin' I like better than goin' home to have a few weeks off, do as I please, go in the yard half-naked, without makeup and without havin' my hair done, or play with the dogs or romp around with the cows." She also creates personal time by traveling anonymously, sans wig and makeup, around her home state with Carl in a station wagon or RV.

Dolly has said that she doesn't like to have maids, housekeepers, or cooks at home but admits that other than loving to cook she has no desire to clean her house and has someone come do it twice a week. She says she is not a good housekeeper, and who can blame her really? She had enough of doing all those chores growing up. Most of the time she doesn't like people in her face or in her house and she wants to be able to walk around in a bathrobe with her hair in a scrunchie without having anyone looking at her or reporting back to the press on how she lives.

Carl has managed to maintain his own privacy by staying off the radar and avoiding being photographed. There is a funny story about Carl working in the front yard when a group of tourists came by and wanted to take some pictures of Dolly's house. They checked with the man working in the yard, who they thought was the gardener. He said he thought it was probably okay and after they took their pictures they thanked him and told him they hoped he wouldn't lose his job!

She feels that home is wherever you feel like you can settle down, be comfortable and safe. At each of her homes she has a chapel or prayer space where she can meditate and pray, and she likes to do all of her songwriting and reading in bed. This is, perhaps, especially important for someone who spends so much time on the road; she has found ways to make herself feel at home wherever she goes.

> "I love to read. I love to cook. I love hanging out with my husband, riding around in our little RV."

City and Country

Close to her heart is what she calls her Tennessee Mountain Home, built on the land where the old home she grew up in used to stand. She had her brother Bobby build it to look like when they were kids but have the house be fully functional—meaning it has all of the modern conveniences. Her mother then came in and decorated it down to the last detail. There is also a replica of the original house at Dollywood that is about the same size.

Dolly says that as much as she loves the country, she loves her some glamour too. At one point she had sixteen homes from the East Coast across to the West Coast, including in Tennessee, New York City, California, and Hawaii. And, of course, several tour buses over the years, which serve as her home on the road.

Willow Lake Plantation is Dolly and Carl's dream house in Brentwood, in horse country outside of Nashville. A twenty-three-room old-fashioned-looking Southern mansion sometimes referred to as "Tara" in the press, after Scarlett O'Hara's childhood home in *Gone with the Wind*, it sits on a large farm set far back from the road. There are several rustic barns, as well as the chapel where she and Carl renewed their vows on their Golden Anniversary. She keeps a bunker on the grounds of her Nashville estate that contains every dress she has ever worn, thousands of them, as well as a building just for her wigs. Her current manager, Danny Nozell, says the costume warehouse is "like a weapons silo. Huge metal doors. You'd need to blow them off to get in there." She also has a lake house nearby, an office complex for her businesses, and an apartment in the Belle Meade section of Nashville.

There is the New York City penthouse apartment on Fifth Avenue with a panoramic view of Central Park that she shared with Sandy Gallin in the 1980s. When Sandy left show business to start buying and designing high-end real estate, she got a separate apartment for herself.

At one time she had three homes in California. One in West Hollywood was the childhood home of Natalie Wood, a 1,000-square-foot cottage that was described in the *Daily Mail* as having "eccentric charm with cactus and country pink gingham and cottage touches." Dolly called it a "whimsical oasis" and lived there when she was filming or working. She also had a little hideaway in the artsy, mountain desert town, Idyllwild, where she and Judy Ogle would sometimes go for girls' weekends and retreats, and a small cottage in the Dutch colony town of Solvang, in the Santa Ynez Valley.

Although, given her traveling for her career, many of the residences are conveniences that allow her to have a home wherever she goes. She says that most of them are investments. She'd rather buy property than play the stock market.

Home Is Your Sanctuary

Dolly lived in trailers, basements, and whatever cheap little places she could find during her first couple of years in Nashville. She and Carl eventually moved into a little house downtown once they were married, but as soon as she started making enough money they bought seventy-five acres of land so they could build their dream house, which became Willow Lake Plantation, where they still live today. Dolly and Carl drew up the floor plans themselves and the house was built by her uncle Dot Watson, Carl, and her brothers Denver and Randy. It took almost two years to build and it was a thrill for Dolly to come home from being on the road to see the progress they were making. They worked incredibly hard and Carl wanted to do it himself as a kind of tribute of his love for her. She thinks that his building that house was the most wonderful gift in the world, better than anything he could have bought. He added a lot of personal touches, like some of the original logs and rocks salvaged from the house Dolly grew up in, and incorporated them in a ground-floor fireplace.

In addition to the antebellum-style mansion, the property also has a guest house, barns, a tennis court, and a swimming pool with a butterfly design at the bottom. The house is set back from the road with a front gate and fence for the sake of privacy. Within the grounds are outbuildings, rolling hills, a little stream, and plenty of space for their horses, dogs, and at one time twenty-five Hereford cows. Peacocks parade around the property.

She wanted her house to be done up "real special" and originally decorated it in pretty pinks and reds, with touches of blue. She filled the house with antiques, including the kitchen table her father had built where they all ate growing up. When she achieved mainstream success, she brought in a decorator from Los Angeles named Bill Lane. While much of it is decorated in signature Dolly Parton country style, it also has a lot of L.A. style, with a few Asian pieces thrown in, including some Buddha statues, which horrified her Christian mother, who considered Buddhas to be false idols.

Of course, given Dolly's extravagant wardrobe, there are a lot of closets, some bigger than others. She has an entire wing above the den devoted to her wardrobe, some twelve closets, larger than the house she grew up in. According to the *Dolly Parton Scrapbook* from the 1970s, she keeps her clothes "organized according to category, throughout the closets with her skirts, dresses, and jeans upstairs and her winter coats and costumes, about three thousand glittery rhinestone covered work outfits, downstairs." Her mama said, back in the late '70s, that she had at least a thousand pairs of shoes and could retire and spend the rest of her life just trying on all of her clothes. That wardrobe has since increased into the tens of thousands.

Her favorite room in the house, given how much she loves to cook, is the kitchen. It is extra large and combines both the most modern appliances with an old country cupboard and wood-burning stove like the one her mother used to have.

The house itself has six large pillars in the front, and upper and lower verandas with rockers on the front porch. She and Carl like to sit there and just hang out and talk or play horseshoes, tend to the animals, do some gardening, go fishing, take walks, or hit tennis balls on the court. There are terrific old photos of Dolly cutting down a tree, of her bundled up on a sled and walking alongside a horse. All good ole down-home pastimes that signify home for her.

With all of her traveling and time on her tour bus, Dolly

is used to life on the road, which is not an easy thing, especially when you are a woman with closets full of wigs and costumes. She says she doesn't even sleep in hotels anymore and there is a special parking spot for her bus at her Dream-More Resort. Even though she has her own luxurious marble hotel suite there, she prefers to stay on the bus in her special spot because it's so comfy and homey!

Over the years, touring all over the country and the world, she has clearly learned what she requires to feel that sense of home and comfort. She travels with her favorite pillows, familiar blankets, candles, Earl Grey tea, her favorite cups, and a fridge full of healthy food—and some good ole Southern comfort food, too, like meat loaf and mashed potatoes, in case she gets a hankering. While these small personal luxuries are set up for her on her tour bus, when she is traveling by plane or camper she also brings those things along packed in her suitcases to make her feel relaxed (minus the meat loaf and mashed potatoes!).

She also knows it's important to have cozy places to sit, especially since she likes to work from her couch or bed. She rises early to pray, write, and get herself organized for the day. She says she does have offices everywhere but she doesn't really use them. She just piles everything onto her bed and has files of her music in every house. She also has a large music room on the first floor of Willow Lake that includes a stage and studio.

Travel in Style: *Dolly I*, *II*, and *III*

Constantly being on the road is no easy task. Early on in her career, when Dolly traveled on her tour bus, the *Coach of Many Colors* with its huge butterfly painted on the side, she was usually the only woman; her band, her manager, and her bus driver were all men. The men slept in bunks and she slept in the back in her own room.

When Dolly started out, she made sure all of her costumes and gowns were wash and wear so she could wash them out in the sink on the bus and hang them to dry. She would bring five or so outfits and five wigs, styled and ready to go. From her early days of touring, she always makes sure there is a little porcelain bathtub surrounded by a shower stand so she can take a bath on the bus!

Over the years she has gone through several buses. *Dolly I*, which was built in 1994, is now on display at Dollywood next to the Chasing Rainbows museum. It was custom built, at 45 feet long, 9 feet wide, and 13.5 feet high, and cost $750,000 to build. It has a generator with enough power to supply the average home with electricity. And it gets seven miles to the gallon with a tank that is big enough to drive the 2,050 miles between Nashville and Los Angeles without stopping. *Dolly I* traveled over 600,000 miles.

When *Dolly I* retired, along came *Dolly II* and, now, *Dolly III*, which cost $2.7 million to build. Dolly's home on wheels has everything she needs on it—a full-size bed with comfy, country-style bedding and pillows; a full-length closet for her clothes and costumes; a cabinet for her wigs; a vanity for her makeup; a full-size fridge; a fully functioning kitchen; and banquettes to sit on. There are also triple bunk beds for Judy and Don and Ann Warden.

As Dolly became more successful and assured in her career, she became more specific about what elements she needed in order to feel at home. For example, in *Dolly I* there are mirrors on the ceiling, because, according to the tour guide at Dollywood, Dolly is claustrophobic, a result of being locked in the closet at school when she was being bullied by the other kids. Her newest bus went a step further and has two side walls that pull out when parked to help create more interior space.

Gypsy Fever

As a kid, all Dolly wanted to do was see the world outside of the Smoky Mountains and all it had to offer. From that first bus ride 200 miles from Pigeon Forge to Nashville to having a tour bus that can drive all night from Nashville to Los Angeles without stopping, she has done what she set out to accomplish. She has traveled all over the United States time and time again, lived in New York and L.A. and Hawaii, and toured all over the world. She travels near and far, whether with Carl to historic little towns close to home or with Sandy

Gallin sailing around Australia. Traveling opens your mind to other cultures, experiences, foods, architecture, traditions, philosophies, and, of course, people. What Dolly has found is that no matter where she goes, people suffer and experience joy and have the same feelings. Her sensitivity to this is one of the reasons she writes songs that feel so universal.

Despite her love of being home to write her songs, poems, and books, she says she was born with gypsy fever and tends to go stir-crazy. For her, staying home all the time can be boring and she is the first to say she was born restless. This is a woman who likes to be on the move.

Even after traveling thousands of miles on tour, she will often go home and say to Carl, "Get the camper; let's go somewhere."

He'll say, "Are you kidding? Ain't you tired of riding?"

"No, I'm a gypsy. I want to do that."

Dolly and Carl love getting in their RV to travel around, usually on the weekends, all over Tennessee and other Southern states within a few hours' drive. Carl loves maps and discovering new places, so they will find "all the little places that are just out of the way and have a little history. Or are just exceptionally beautiful. And sometimes we just get a wild hair and say 'Let's drive down to Graceland.'" They've gone to Tupelo, Mississippi, to see Elvis's childhood home and Carl Perkins's childhood home. She loves to see other well-known people's houses because she thinks you can learn a lot about them by seeing what their childhood was like.

Of course, part of the fun of traveling around in a camper is living close to the earth and being able to cook or eat outdoors. There is a wonderful old photo of Dolly crouching down on a campsite blanket covered with food—you can see a bottle of barbecue sauce—with a lit lantern in the center. You can just imagine her heating up the enamel kettle over a campfire to make a cup of Earl Grey tea.

Dolly loves to have a good picnic. In 1977 she completely befuddled Chet Flippo when she took him on a picnic during an interview. As they drove around, looking for a spot to throw down their blanket and have their bologna and tomato sandwiches and cheap wine, she suggested a cemetery.

When they got settled, she stretched her arms out and proclaimed, "Oh, I just love it outdoors. You can just feel God all around you."

This was not some savvy young star trying to charm a journalist by showing him how down-to-earth she was. When she was a child mourning the loss of her baby brother, she used to sleep outside on his grave. She said she likes to write in graveyards because they are so peaceful and conducive to introspection. Being a country girl, spending time outdoors feels like home to her, and camping and having picnics are some of her favorite things to do. On the weekends she will cook at home; make up a basket of Carl's favorite foods and treats, like fried Cornish hens, homemade potato salad, and green beans; and they will put it in their camper and go for a drive, picking up some iced tea on the road. They can throw their blanket down on a riverbank, go fishing if they like, and enjoy the peace and quiet, good food, nature, and each other's company. It's very romantic if you don't mind the bugs and bears.

Be a Matriarch

Dolly always felt that, when she was growing up, women were the ones who kept everything together. Even though Dolly never had children of her own, five of her younger siblings lived with her as soon as she had her own house in Nashville, and all of her nieces and nephews call her "Aunt Granny."

When Dolly and Carl got married, she just assumed they would have kids and "weren't doing anything to stop it." They had names picked out and everything. "My husband and I, when we first got married, we thought about if we had kids, what would they look like? Would they be tall—because he's tall? Or would they be little squats like me? If we'd had a girl, she was gonna be called Carla...Anyway, we talked about it, and we dreamed it, but it wasn't meant to be."

As sad as she was when she had her partial hysterectomy and realized she was never going to be a mother herself, her philosophy was, "God didn't mean for me to have kids so everybody's kids could be mine." She realized that if she had kids, she would have probably been like her mama and sisters and given up her other dreams to be a mother. If she had kids, she probably wouldn't have become a star.

She regularly hosts not only her siblings but also her many nieces and nephews, and grandnieces and grandnephews, of all ages. "I live on a farm. They love to come out with me. We get on a golf cart and go all over the place." She isn't one to have glamorous celebrity parties at home but she sure takes care of her very large, very extended family.

As soon as the house was built, Dolly and Carl moved her younger siblings in to raise them, give them a good place to live, and help out her mama and daddy. Her sister Cassie has lived and worked with her for most of her life. She also took in the twins, Freida and Floyd; Rachel; and occasionally Randy when he wasn't out on the road playing music. Stella, who is a singer and songwriter in her own right, came and really took care of everything and everybody when Dolly was out on the road.

"What is more important than your family?" she asks. "Even if you don't like 'em—some you don't—you love them...When the chips are down and something really bad happens, you realize how important it is to have family around. I am from a rich background. It made me really embrace that and to encourage other people to embrace that. Don't ever be ashamed of your family, your sexual orientation or your nationality. Be who you are."

Dolly has said there is nothing better than creating family traditions and sitting around a big table with each other to eat, laugh, tell jokes, sing, and just enjoy each other.

Stone Soup

One of the family traditions in the Parton household was Mama's stone soup. The story behind it is told in Dolly's books and also shown in the movie *Coat of Many Colors*. When Dolly was growing up, most of the ingredients came from the family's farm but sometimes there wasn't enough meat for the soup. Mama would tell the children the legend of stone soup and send them out to the yard for each to find their own perfect rock to scrub and polish. Whichever child was feeling most out of sorts that day would get chosen to put their special rock in the soup. Avie Lee would say that it was the stone that gave the soup its special flavor. The special stone was that little something extra to take the children's mind off their hunger and their troubles.

Ingredients

Olive oil
1 small onion, chopped
2 large carrots, diced
4 garlic cloves, minced
1 very clean stone
1 pound russet potatoes, peeled and diced
1 pound turnips, peeled and diced
1 small head cabbage, coarsely chopped
1 (14½ ounce) can diced tomatoes
1 smoked ham hock, if available

2 quarts chicken stock or canned low-sodium broth
Salt and pepper

Directions

Cover the bottom of a large soup pot with olive oil and sauté onion, carrots, and garlic until soft. Place the special stone in the bottom of the pot. Add potatoes, turnips, cabbage, and tomatoes to the pot and stir. Add ham hock and stock and reduce heat to low and simmer, stirring occasionally, until the soup thickens and the vegetables are tender, about two hours. Remove the ham hock from the soup, remove the meat from the bone, and chop it into ½-inch pieces, then add the meat back to the soup. Season to taste with the salt and pepper. Serve hot.

Christmas, of course, is a huge holiday for her and she celebrates several times, with part of her family in Nashville, then East Tennessee, and with her husband's family at their home. "My people celebrate on Christmas Eve and open presents, and his celebrate on Christmas Day." Before Christmas, she goes into a "happy frenzy" and starts cooking some of her favorite dishes, like biscuits, pecan chicken salad, pimento cheese sandwiches, holiday ham, chicken and dumplings, and all sorts of pies.

A week before Christmas, she will host what she calls Granny Night, and dress up in a red velvet suit as "Granny Claus" and has all of the kids come over. She will "load up the table with all kinds of homemade goodies: thumbprint cookies, Hello Dolly bars, walnut candy and kettle corn. Then I come in carrying a big sack of presents. 'Ho ho ho!' I belt out. The kids go crazy. I don't know who has more fun, them or me."

Have Southern Hospitality

Being friendly and making people comfortable is true of Southern people in general and certainly a big part of Dolly's makeup. She is known as the "hostess" of Dollywood and has tried to create a friendly atmosphere that is accepting of all people, where anyone can feel at home. Being hospitable is just about making people feel welcome. It's the way she was raised and the environment she tries to create both at home and with her businesses. Southern hospitality is just that good-ole welcome-home feeling where you can pull up a chair, take a load off, drink some sweet tea, and relax with family and friends.

A big part of Southern hospitality, of course, is food—not just the eating of it but the preparing of it. Dolly says that when she is home, "everybody wants to be in the kitchen. I think it goes back to mothers. When I was a little girl, I always wanted to be in the kitchen because it was warm and that's where my mother was. You never lose that feeling." Her favorite meal for entertaining is roast pork, green beans, turnip greens, and fried okra. And as any good Southerner knows, when it comes to food, the greasier the better.

Everyone knows the old party conversation starter "If you could invite any five people throughout history, living or dead, to dinner, who would it be?" When journalist Lawrence Grobel asked Dolly that question, and asked what she would cook for them, she named Will Rogers, Beethoven, Bob Hope, Strother Martin, and the character Festus from *Gunsmoke*, although she didn't provide any explanations. Interesting, isn't it, that she wanted to fill her table with talented and witty men! She said she would make them "fried potatoes and green beans, country style creamed corn, corn bread and biscuits, pinto beans and turnip greens, meat loaf. I'd probably make up a vanilla pudding. I'd have to fix Beethoven a chef's salad. I don't think he'd want all that grease."

Dolly loves to cook and published two cookbooks, *Dolly's Dixie Fixin's* and *Tennessee Mountain Home Cooking*. Despite her diets and struggles with weight, she loves good old-fashioned country cooking, like she grew up with. Biscuits and gravy, fried chicken, fried pork chops, fried okra, fried anything! She told Andy Warhol her specialties are chicken and dumplings and poke sallet, which is cooked greens made from pokeweed. She is known to dole them out to neighbors and family in Tupperware containers during holidays. And she is apparently famous for her spaghetti, which biographer Alanna Nash said was unlike any other she had ever had. Dolly makes the sauce herself and puts a ton of vegetables in it so that it is almost like a stew on top of the noodles.

RECIPES

....

Chicken and Dumplin's

Ingredients

CHICKEN:

1 chicken, approximately 3 pounds, or two full chicken breasts
 (if you prefer white meat)

1 onion, peeled and left whole

¼ cup chopped celery leaves

2 teaspoons salt

¾ teaspoon black pepper

Directions

Put the chicken and 2 teaspoons of salt in 2 quarts of water in a Dutch oven. Cover the chicken and wait for the water to come to a boil.

Once the water boils, turn the temperature down to medium heat. Add the onion, celery leaves, and ¾ teaspoon of black pepper.

Let the chicken simmer until the meat falls off the bone.

Take the chicken and onion out of the cooking pot and fish out the celery leaves with a strainer and throw them away, along with the onion, leaving the broth.

Let the chicken cool, then cut the meat into 1-inch pieces. Discard any skin and bones left over.

Bring the chicken broth back to high heat and allow to boil.

Ingredients

DUMPLINGS:

2 cups all-purpose flour, plus extra for kneading

½ teaspoon baking soda

½ teaspoon salt

3 tablespoons vegetable shortening

¾ cup milk

Directions

Mix the flour, baking soda, and ½ teaspoon of salt together in a bowl, then cut the shortening into small pieces with a pastry cutter or food processor. Add the shortening and stir until the mixture is a breadcrumb-like consistency.

Stir in the milk slowly so the dough is slightly moist, then spread it out on a flour-covered surface and knead for 5 minutes. Roll the dough into a ½-inch thickness, then cut into 1½-inch squares.

Add the dough squares to the boiling broth. Reduce to low heat, cover the pot, and let simmer for about 10 minutes, stirring occasionally.

Add chicken to the pot and cook for several minutes until the chicken is warmed all the way through, then serve hot.

Glazed Baked Ham with Pineapple and Honey

Ingredients

1 fully cooked bone-in ham
Whole cloves
1 can sliced pineapple, including juice
1 cup light brown sugar, packed
2 tablespoons vinegar
1 teaspoon Dijon mustard

Directions

Preheat oven to 325 degrees.

Bake ham according to package instructions, discarding the prepackaged glaze that comes with the ham. Using a knife, remove the skin and score a diamond pattern into the fat with each slice being around 1 inch. Insert a clove into each diamond and then cook ham in a roasting pan. Remove ham 30 minutes before done.

While the ham cooks, make the glaze in a small saucepan, mixing pineapple juice from can, brown sugar, vinegar, and mustard over medium-high heat and gently boiling. Remove from burner and brush the ham with glaze and put pineapple slices around the ham in the roasting pan before putting back into the oven for the remaining 30 minutes.

When done, remove the bone from the ham, discard cloves, and slice. Place on platter and drizzle again with glaze. Serve remaining glaze on the side.

Fried Okra

Ingredients

1 pound okra
¾ cups stoneground cornmeal
½ cup flour
½ teaspoon salt
Canola oil, for frying

Directions

Preheat oven to 350 degrees.

Wash okra and cut into ½-inch rounds. Mix together okra, cornmeal, flour, and salt in a large mixing bowl or large plastic bag and shake around to coat the okra evenly.

Fill a large heavy-bottomed Dutch oven or cast-iron skillet with 1 inch canola oil and set it over high heat until the point that, if a drop of water is added, it will sizzle.

Allow okra to brown on one side, about 3 minutes, before gently stirring. Once both sides of okra have browned, about 3 more minutes, place into preheated oven. Cook until fork tender, about 10 minutes.

Salt additionally if desired.

Hello Dolly Bars/Magic Cookie Bars

Ingredients

8 tablespoons (1 stick) butter, melted
1 cup graham cracker crumbs
½ cup chocolate chips
½ cup butterscotch chips
1 cup sweetened shredded or flaked coconut
1 cup chopped nuts, preferably pecans
1 (14-ounce) can sweetened condensed milk

Directions

Preheat the oven to 350 F.

Pour the melted butter into an 8-by-8-inch baking pan. Spread the graham cracker crumbs in the bottom of the pan in an even layer. Arrange the chocolate and butterscotch chips over the crumbs, followed by the coconut and pecans. Press down with a fork. Feel free to add as many layers as you like. When done layering, pour the condensed milk over the pecans. Bake until golden, about 20 minutes. The bars will not look like they're cooked; they need to cool on a rack to firm up. Once cooled, slice into bars and serve.

WWDD TO CREATE A SENSE OF HOME?

- Maintain your privacy and let your home time be about rest, relaxation, and recharging with people you love.
- Create a sense of home wherever you are with your personal creature comforts.
- Enjoy the outdoors, whether packing a picnic, camping, hiking, swimming, fishing, or just sitting on the front porch.
- Nurture maternal instincts whether you have children or not by creating family traditions and making others feel at home.
- Cook comfort food and enjoy it with friends and family.

Chapter Nine

God, Sex, and Music

Create Your Own Form of Spirituality

Dolly has her own unique brand of spirituality that has guided her since she was a young child and provided the conviction, resilience, faith, and determination that allowed her to reach for her dreams and higher purpose. Her strong faith and wisdom inspired some of her friends to give her the nickname the "Dolly Mama."

Dolly's maternal grandfather was a Pentecostal preacher, the pastor of their church, the House of Prayer, and he scared the heck out of her. Her daddy's side was Baptist. Her mother taught her Bible stories and provided a strong sense of faith, purpose, and spiritual responsibility. When she was a child, a woman who was considered a saint or prophet put her hands on Dolly in church and said, "This child is anointed." Her mother told Dolly that it meant God had special plans for her and that she was meant to go out and help people. As a result, Dolly felt it was her destiny to leave the farm and go out into the world to preach, but through music. She has said that if she hadn't become a singer and songwriter that she would have become a beautician or a preacher.

In her autobiography, she tells the story of how her strong faith was sealed, in what may seem to be unconventional circumstances. She said that her three passions were always God, sex, and music, not necessarily in that order. In a way the three have always been intertwined for her. She would spend time as a twelve-year-old girl in a run-down, abandoned church in her community where she would talk to God. It is there that she had a spiritual awakening. At the time she was confused about religion, about sexuality, and about who she was in the world. The church had a broken-down piano and she used the keys and strings to make music. It was also where the teenagers would go to have sex, and there were dirty pictures on the wall and used condoms on the floor. As she tells it, "I would sing hymns to God for a while and look at dirty pictures for a while and pray for a while and one day as I prayed in earnest, I broke through some sort of spirit wall and found God." She realized that she could be a sexual being and still be a God-respecting person. One did not have to exclude the other. And music was her way of expressing her love for both of those things. The seemingly contradictory parts of her nature did not need to be kept separate.

She may have grown up with holy rollers, but she has created her own form of spirituality that involves a deep faith in a traditional Judeo-Christian God but doesn't necessarily follow religion, despite quoting Scripture as inspiration. She says, "I've learned through the years to communicate with

God as I perceive him. I pray for guidance and I accept the things that come as an answer to prayers."

In the mid-'70s Dolly told journalist Alanna Nash her thoughts on religion, explaining that she knew the Bible inside and out and found it fascinating but that, despite believing in God, being baptized, and having such a religious upbringing, she didn't consider herself a Christian. "I would like to think I have a Christian outlook on life as far as the way I treat people. I feel like that one wrong thing you do to somebody else is a sin. But for me to say I'm a good Christian, I would have to be devotin' the same kind of time to God and giving him all my efforts the way that I am with this business."

Preach, Dolly, preach! We are listening.

"We all need to have hope that there's something bigger than we are. Even if I knew for a fact that there was no God, I'd still believe."

Saint Dolly

One day Carl was on the set of *9 to 5*, speaking to Jane Fonda, and when Jane paid Dolly a compliment, saying how easy she was to work with, Carl came back with, "Well, she's an angel," and Jane said, "Yes, she is," to which he responded, "No, you don't get it; she's a real angel."

There's no question that music is healing, and music fans will often compare seeing one of their favorite musicians in concert with going to church. What makes Dolly and her music stand out is that she appears to have an almost otherworldly spirit that goes beyond her ability to create moving performances. Three particularly successful journalists were all deeply affected by her spiritual presence and felt compelled to write about it. It's almost too much of a coincidence.

Chet Flippo, in his second 1977 interview with Dolly for *Rolling Stone*, wrote the following:

> I have heard singers called many things, from four-letter words to 27-letter words, but I have never heard one called a "purifier"...But came one recent Friday morning when my own purifying sleep was disturbed by a phone call. I dispatched my helpmate to deal with it, but couldn't help overhearing her end of the conversation, which was mostly astonished gasps. "What was all that about?" I asked. It was, I was told, an editor of a certain women's magazine and she was just calling to inform us that Dolly Parton had "purified" New York's Bottom Line the night before.
>
> "What'd she do, take an ax to the place?"
>
> "No, her music purified the audience. She's a purifier."

Well, damn me. I have known Dolly Parton for some time and known her as someone who writes a hell of a good country song and sings with an achingly sweet soprano and looks like what heaven should be populated with. But I also know her as a good ol' girl you can kid around with and not have to be too careful of what you do or say. Hardly someone, though, to get all misty eyed or mystical over or go sobbing about in night clubs. Further callers throughout the day, however, report similar quasi-religious experiences and cleansings of the soul.

By the end of the lengthy article, however, Chet finds himself teary eyed and feeling "purified" himself at one of her concerts.

In 1980, Roger Ebert interviewed Dolly one-on-one and many years later shared the following story:

As we spoke, I found myself enveloped by her presence. This had nothing to do with sex appeal. Far from it. It was as if I were being mesmerized by a benevolent power. I left the room in a cloud of good feeling. Next day, Siskel and I were sitting next to each other on an airplane. "This will sound crazy," he said, "but when I was interviewing Dolly Parton, I almost felt like she had healing powers."

Lawrence Grobel, who knew Dolly for many years and interviewed her several times for *Playboy*, *Playgirl*, and *Ladies' Home Journal*, said of her:

> It's almost as if she is more than human. Her intelligence is obvious and overwhelming. Her sense of things—of knowing things about people—is uncanny. She has a certain strength and confidence that is deeply spiritual. She's just so damn different from anybody else—a self-created creature with an enormous talent and a heart just as big.

Her understanding of human nature, her honesty, and her humanity can seem otherworldly and nudge open even the most difficult of souls. Dolly's own explanation is that "I love everybody and I go right through the bullshit and I go right to the core of every person because we are all one. We are all the same."

You Gotta Have Faith

Dolly's belief in God is an essential part of who she is, and she credits it with making her so successful and helping her maintain her success: "You have to believe in something bigger than yourself. We grew up believing that through God all things are possible. I think I believed that so much that I made it happen."

When she was a child, there was a man who came to visit her school and gave out key chains with a picture of a mustard seed and a Bible verse on it: "If ye have faith, even as much as a single seed of mustard, ye shall be able to move mountains." That day the man told a story of someone who, after reading that Scripture, stayed up all night praying that the mountain outside of his house would move to the other side of the house before the next morning. The next day he looked out the window and saw that the mountain hadn't moved and said, "See there. I knew it!" Dolly says that this was a case of "faith working in the negative" and that she always knew that her dreams would come true. And that man didn't. It is a self-fulfilling prophecy. The difference is in the level of faith you have. Matthew 17:20 has become Dolly's favorite Scripture. She specifically loves the last line, which says, "Nothing will be impossible for you."

Her grandfather Jake Owens was the inspiration for her song "The Old Time Preacher Man." She remembers "the hellfire and brimstone he used to preach and how I used to be *real* scared of that and I think that inspired me or *depressed* me into writin' all these sad, mournful songs. You kind of grew up in a horrid atmosphere about fear of religion. We thought God was a *monster* in the sky."

Dolly's fundamentalist, Scripture-based, country-style religion did not turn her into a religious fanatic, and while her spirituality has diverged at times from her upbringing, there are two fundamental tenets that she lives by to this day: She believes in something greater, and she always tries to find the good in everything and everybody.

The song she wrote that could be called the closest to gospel is "The Seeker." In it she struggles through her own conflicted feelings about religion. She says as much as she feels that God is the best friend she has in the world, but she just can't commit to calling herself a Christian. "I was out in the kitchen a-cookin' and I started thinkin' about how serious that was, so—I am a seeker, a poor sinful creature, there is none weaker than I am, I am a seeker and you are a teacher. So I was just thinkin', 'Lord, you're gonna have to hit me with a bolt of lightning because I ain't gonna do it on my own.' So I wrote that out of a heavy heart. Because I am certainly not a Christian. I will try *some* of *anything*, I mean I will."

She decided she could not believe in a God that was mean or cruel. She had to figure out who she was and what God meant to her. She feels that you need to get in touch with God and your own subconscious—the two are inseparable: "While Christianity and its symbols are a big part of my own life, I am not one of those who believes that a person has to embrace them to be a decent and worthwhile person." To Dolly, spirituality and its expression are a deeply personal matter. As a result, she has a close and personal relationship with God and feels that her positive attitude and her inner strength come from it. She feels like she has a higher purpose in life, what she calls a "divinely inspired and ordained mission." And she distinguishes between spirituality and religion. She feels that religion can be so organized and categorized that it can "lose sight of the true love of the spirit."

Find Your God Spark

Dolly calls that inner beauty and love that can shine and make other people feel good her "God spark" and says, "I really do ask God every single day to let me do something, say something, be something that matters to somebody else. To make somebody feel good. To let people see a spark of love." She will look in the mirror and talk to Him, looking into her own eyes, searching for that higher wisdom to come through.

Finding that extra light in yourself, your God-given gifts—which can be a talent, an ability, or just your essential goodness or Godlike nature—and using them for the greater good is your "God spark." Connecting to that God spark inside of you allows you to share it with others. Dolly prays every day that "God will lead me and direct me and bring all the right, the good, things in, take all the wrong, the bad, things out."

Dolly sees music as her way to spread light and joy and faith to others. She calls it her "ministry" and hopes it lifts people up. Every Sunday and at church events during the week, the Partons would all bring their musical instruments—banjos, tambourines, fiddles, guitars—and they would get up and sing. They sang old hymns and most of the service was a combination of Bible teachings and song. Church was a social event and it was not just Sunday service but revivals, prayer meetings, and evening services. It was very casual and in the simplest of buildings, and their biggest form of recreation. But music was also one of the primary ways that they expressed their joys and sorrows and faith in God. Dolly's example proves we could all work toward bringing the light we have inside and sharing it with the world, in whatever capacity or form works best for us—preacher, singer, writer, artist, inventor, mother, teacher. Whatever it is that helps you share your gifts with others is an expression of your own spiritual life.

In turn, it is just as important to try to see the good and God in others, no matter how different they may be from yourself. Easier said than done but it all starts with an open mind and an open heart. That empathy and understanding of a common humanity is something we could all use a little bit more of. Look for the best in every person and encourage it.

Prayer and Meditation

Dolly prays and meditates every day and feels it is the secret to her incredible energy. Whether it's at the small chapel at her office complex or what she calls her "pray-do" at her New York City apartment, she gets down on her knees to pray. She also does walking prayer and meditation.

She manages to hold it together in dark times, attributing it to knowing "I've got help whenever everybody else might seem not to be there for me. I always know that God is there.

And I can talk to Him and always seem to feel better and know the right answers. I never make a decision about business or anything without talkin' to God about it, and usually when I do, I feel after I pray that I've got my answer."

That close relationship or feeling of direct contact is something she has always felt inside of her. As a child, instead of having imaginary friends to talk to or play with, she had imaginary angels. This feeling of having the protection of a higher power gets her through, keeping her constantly in touch with herself and confident in the decisions and choices she is making, and helps her know where in her life she needs to ask for help or express gratitude.

Even though things may not be going the way you want, see what it is you've got and stay open to the twists and turns of life. When the chips are down, pray for guidance. Pray for wisdom. Then listen when that guidance and wisdom show up. They may not show up in the way you want or expect, so pay close attention. As Dolly says, "God doesn't set too many bushes on fire in front of you," so listen to your heart and reach for your inner wisdom. Obviously, if He does set a bush on fire in front of you, you'd better do whatever He tells you to. That's not the sort of thing you want to mess with.

And speaking of bushes, burning or not, Dolly grew up knowing the beauty and fury of nature—from snowstorms, to Tennessee twisters, to beetles attacking the tobacco crops that were the family's livelihood—and the importance of respecting it. An appreciation of nature and its strength as well as its gentleness is an important part of a spiritual life. Nature is God's church and its beauty and energy can get you out of a rut, help solve a creative problem, or just help you relax.

Who hasn't felt better, more connected to the earth, after planting, nurturing, and caring for their own garden, lying down in the grass to watch the twinkling stars, chasing fireflies or butterflies, hiking through the woods, jumping into a lake or river, or breathing in the fresh mountain or ocean air?

As a child, Dolly would wander off by herself to go write or just lie down in a field to watch the clouds floating by, imagining they were all sorts of things. The endless variety and beauty of the great outdoors is something she enjoys and finds meditative and soothing. She thinks of all of it as "God's coloring book." The many sounds of the Smoky Mountains—the rain, the streams, the birds, the wind—all of nature's music preceded man's music. She sees music as mimicking the original sounds God created in the natural world. And so spending time there makes you closer to God, as well as being inspiring.

At her Chasing Rainbows museum, there is a plaque on the wall with one of her quotes: "I have never ceased to be amazed by nature. Anybody who spends any time at all observing nature has to believe there is a God." Take time to get out of your head and into your bare feet and appreciate the beauty of the world around you. You never know what kind of inspiration and sense of wonder it will create in you.

Go on a Spiritual Retreat

Dolly takes time out from her regular schedule to have spiritual fasts where she spends a few days alone focusing only on prayer, meditation, her goals, her dreams, or her problems with specific people or situations. She also spends time counting her blessings and being grateful for all of the good things that are happening in her life. She often does this at her Tennessee Mountain home but sometimes takes Judy along, especially when she feels run-down or has a problem she needs to solve. They will drive to one of her homes in California, or go to the mountains or the ocean, where they will disappear from the outside pressures of the world for a few days or a few weeks. They make elaborate lists, pray on them, and do affirmations.

Dolly likes to read Scripture that seems appropriate to whatever challenge she is facing. Her two favorite prayers to say are the Lord's Prayer and Psalm 23, which begins with "The Lord is my shepherd, I shall not want..." Of course, your own spiritual retreat is for you to design, and you can pray or meditate or read whatever material inspires you or just contemplate life as you go on a hike. These types of retreats, whether they are for an hour or a month, can help you connect to your own higher purpose and help you find the ways to overcome obstacles and create paths for fulfilling your own dreams.

Halos and Horns

Dolly acknowledges that everyone has a little bit of angel and a little bit of devil in them—it's human nature. "I feel that sin and evil are the negative part of you and I think it's like a battery: you've got to have the negative and the positive in order to be a complete person."

She certainly isn't above indulging her devil side from time to time: "I'm one of the world's sinners. I think I'm a vanilla sinner—too bad to be good and too good to be bad. Because it wouldn't be *all* that hard to be good but I just don't know that I *want* to be. I think I won't have no fun if I'm *too* good. "That is why I try to say, 'I'm no angel.' I'm capable of doing things," she says. "What I ain't done, I might do yet."

She knows that in an era of celebrity worship, it is easy to fall into arrogance or thinking you are better than others. She does not want to be idolized and knows that we are all just human. She loves and takes care of her family, she is proud of where she comes from, and she respects God. This humility is a big part of why she remains so down-to-earth, so open and accessible.

When she went through her depression in the early '80s and was not working, she hit a low point that led to an epiphany. She kept a gun in the nightstand next to her bed in case of burglars. One day she sat there, looking at the gun. She recalls, "I looked at it a long time, wondering and saying to myself, 'Well now, this is where people get the idea of suicide isn't it? Guns around the house and people sorrowing and all.' Then, just as I picked it up, just to hold it and look at it for a moment, our little dog Popeye came running up the stairs. The tap-tap-tap of his paws jolted me back to reality. I suddenly froze. I put the gun down. Then I prayed. I kinda believe Popeye was a spiritual messenger from God." It gave her some wisdom, tolerance, and patience for the struggles of other people. That moment woke her up, in a sense, and from that point on she focused on getting better, getting her career back, losing weight, and creating the spiritual strength to make sure she never hit that kind of bottom again.

Like everyone, she is just trying to do the best she can. The fact is, no one is perfect and we all struggle to balance our angel and devil natures. The more we realize this is just the state of things, the more we can forgive ourselves for our faults and embrace our own fallibility.

Listen to Your (or Someone Else's) Sixth Sense

Dolly's mother had surprisingly accurate premonitions, and the entire family knew better than to ignore Avie's sixth sense, which was a God-given gift that was both a blessing and a curse. Dolly's sister Willadeene wrote that Avie had ESP and that things just came to her, in a voice, and she listened. She instinctively knew whether something—a person, a business venture—was going to go wrong or go right for her children and would advise them. She also foresaw many of the tragedies the family would experience.

When she was pregnant with Larry, Dolly's little brother, she knew he wasn't going to live and indeed he died only a few hours after being born. One night she dreamed of something "dark and devouring," which showed up the next day in the form of worms eating their tobacco plants, almost killing the crops and the family's livelihood for a year.

Dolly's own keen understanding of human nature has given her an uncanny ability to read people. She is extremely intuitive and uses that gift in every part of her life. While she doesn't claim to have ESP like her mother, she does listen to her inner voice, whether you want to call it intuition, her soul, or a higher being. Her manager, Danny Nozell, says, "She thinks about things, she prays on them, then she makes a decision. And the decisions more often than not go her way." The more in touch you are with your own inner voice, the more things will go *your* way.

Given her mother's strong sixth sense, Dolly knows to heed spiritual messages when they show up. She told a friend that once, when she was about to board a plane, she saw her grandma's ghost standing in the corner telling her not to get on the plane. It frightened her and she didn't take that flight, changing her ticket. The plane later crashed, killing everyone on board.

Dolly says that both of her grandmothers speak to her from the beyond and provide messages, such as to not sign a contract that may end up costing her millions of dollars. Because of this, Dolly isn't afraid of dying: "I know there is life after death because I speak to my grandmothers."

Dolly often saw faith healings and other miracles as a child. Being so poor, they couldn't always go out and get a doctor if one of them was sick; she remembers "my mom and my grandpa laying hands on the kids, and yes, I have seen some wonderful things. I have seen prayers answered. I grew up that way and I have a lot of faith."

One time there was a huge blizzard, and Dolly, her mother, and all the kids were trapped in their house and couldn't get out. Their father wasn't home at the time and they ran out of food and had no more wood for heat. They almost froze to death but prayed and prayed and managed to survive. She put this story in the TV movie *Christmas of Many Colors* and describes it as a "Christmas miracle and it is about how miraculous prayer is."

There was also a time when Avie Lee got spinal meningitis and her fever was so high they had to pack her in ice. The doctor came and said he didn't think she was going to make it until the next morning. Everyone stayed up and prayed for her all night and she miraculously lived, waking up the next morning asking for some water. She went deaf in one ear, but she also made it into medical books as the woman who survived an unsurvivable fever. She told everyone that she had a textbook near-death experience of going through a tunnel and finding light at the end of it but she heard her children crying for her and came back.

Dolly says she also had a similar out-of-body experience when she was young, where, one day while just hanging out in the grass staring at the sky, she inexplicably felt like she was up in the clouds, looking down on herself. She got scared and went back into her body but ever since then she never feared death. And she has admitted that she has seen and experienced strange happenings that she thinks can only be ghosts.

Dolly is a big believer in God having a larger plan for her that drives her every move. She has said, "All of my life, there has been this strange thing about me. A thing that I can feel; it's almost as if it's something within me that says, 'Do this and that.' The part of my career that looks like plannin' is the part that's already planned out for me. It's just like it's there. I don't try to outstep or outdo it; I wait until I feel it. It's not an actual voice, or an actual thing I can see. But even as a very small, young child, I knew when I should walk in a room. I knew when I should exit. I knew when I should be somewhere when I was wanted; I knew when I was not. I knew the right things to say and do to get out. See, I don't know what it is. That's why I say it's a God-given thing."

While there is no way to expect or create a miracle, you know one when it happens. Given life's struggles, believing that there is more to life than meets the eye—whether it is a belief in the afterlife or the power of prayer—provides optimism and hope. Hope, optimism, love—sometimes they are all we've got and to deny them is to deny some of the magic that can be found in existence.

Acknowledging the mysteries of life and the miracles, both big and small, makes us pause and appreciate the bigger picture. There is pleasure, faith, and solace to be found in the smaller day-to-day miracles of life as well. The more in touch you are with your own God spark, the more you will be aware of them.

WWDD TO NURTURE HER SPIRITUAL LIFE?

- Have a strong belief in something bigger than yourself and through your faith believe that all things are possible.
- Find your God spark and let people see it shine through you.
- Try to see the good and God in others.
- Pray, meditate, go on spiritual retreats, and spend time in nature to work through your problems, choices, and decisions.
- Honor the good and bad in yourself and others and be forgiving toward both.
- Listen to spiritual messages.

Chapter Ten

A Coat of Many Colors

Creativity and Intellectual Pursuits

*I*t's redundant at this point to say that Dolly is an intensely creative and curious person whose rich and varied career has gone far beyond being a country music singer. This is a woman with big ideas and the ability to turn those ideas into reality, as songs, as businesses, as entertainment, as education. She's a honky-tonk version of a Renaissance woman.

Her grandfather answered the question of how long Dolly has been singing with, "Why ever since she quit cryin'. That thing come here a-singin'." And with that singing came her songwriting, which she started before she even attended school, with her mother jotting down the lyrics to her songs. She had a very early song, written when she was about five, called "Life Doesn't Mean That Much to Me," that was a preview of some of the darker, morbid songs of her early career.

She would "make up songs about stories I heard, personal things I heard people say, about feelings and emotions."

She has produced thousands of songs with a working catalog of over three thousand. As we know, she says that coming up with melodies and lyrics is her therapy and her way of working through her feelings and things that are going on in her life. But don't make the mistake of thinking that her songs are strictly autobiographical. She has a far more universal approach to human emotion and experience. She finds inspiration everywhere.

There is no question that Dolly is a prodigy. Even if she did start out with just a homemade mandolin, she went on to learn to play a variety of instruments: guitar, dulcimer, banjo, piano, recorder, harp, harmonica, penny whistle, and saxophone. She says that she plays a little bit of everything. She is self-taught and never formally learned how to read music.

She has said of her songs, "They're my children. I hope to have them support me when I'm old."

As a naturally born creative person with a distinct talent and point of view, it was also crucial to her that she have creative independence. For Dolly, musical and creative freedom go hand in hand with her intellectual freedom. Her one-of-a-kind, straight-from-the-heart approach to life and broad-minded philosophy deeply inform who she is and how she expresses herself.

The extent of her creative powers deserves repeating and her ability to generate ideas and see them come to fruition takes many forms: songwriter, singer, musician, performer, actress, writer/author, film and television producer, Broadway show writer, theme park and dinner theater developer, storyteller, and teller of tall tales. How can the rest of us tap into our creativity and broaden our intellectual horizons following her example, even when we're not nearly as talented? Let's see how she does it.

> "We didn't have television and our radio was used only to listen to the Grand Ole Opry each week and the news. Mama was our entertainment. She sang, she read the Bible to us and she showed us how to cook and sew and make something out of nothing. And I'm still doing that."

Southern Gothic

True to Dolly's Appalachian roots and all of the Elizabethan ballads and ghost stories Avie Lee told, as well as her fire-and-brimstone upbringing, Dolly's early songs addressed some pretty dark themes and taboo subjects. Abandoned children, young girls being betrayed by men who had gotten them pregnant, the shame and consequences women are left to suffer when they go astray, murder, death, drunkenness, suicide, and mental illness all show up in her writing:

"**Me and Little Andy**," the flip side of her big crossover hit "Here You Come Again," is a heartbreaking story of a little girl dressed in rags, holding a puppy, who knocks on the narrator's door in a storm, begging for food and shelter. Her mama had run away again and her daddy was off drunk somewhere. The narrator takes her in and both the girl and the dog die during the night.

"**Jeannie's Afraid of the Dark**" is about a little girl who is afraid of the dark and begs her parents not to bury her when she dies. Her parents don't realize until it's too late that she was predicting her own death, and when she dies of illness, they put an eternal flame on her grave.

"**Evening Shade**" tells the story of an abusive home for orphaned juvenile delinquents who take revenge by burning the place down with the house matron inside of it.

"**Down from Dover**" is about a young woman who is taken advantage of by a man she loves, gets pregnant, and is thrown out of the house by her parents and abandoned. Her baby daughter is stillborn.

"**The Bridge**" is about a pregnant girl abandoned by her lover. She commits suicide by jumping off the bridge where the two consummated their relationship.

"**Daddy Come and Get Me**" tells of a young woman who begs her father to come and get her out of the mental institution that her husband/lover put her in after he leaves her.

Be a Woman of Many Colors

It isn't just songs that she writes. Over the years, Dolly has often talked about countless other things she was writing or planned on writing: self-help books, children's books, short stories, a Broadway show about her life, volumes of poetry, movie scripts, and, of course, her own memoirs. "I've got trunkfuls of things I've written. I've been writin' poetry since I was in grammar school. When I was a teenager, I wrote a lot of *real* hot and heavy love stories." Some of these have seen the light of day and others, we can only hope, will someday be revealed in the Dolly Parton archives.

She is a big-idea person and says, "I love thinking. I love coming up with great ideas. I just get excited. Sometimes if I get a big idea, I'm just like a kid, like I've found a new toy. I love to make things happen, I love to see things happen, I love to be a part of things that are happening."

Dolly says that she gets her ideas from her everyday experiences, things she sees and hears about from her family or friends, things that she reads—like the newspapers that lined the walls of her childhood home—and sometimes, just conversations with other people.

When she is writing, she really dives deep into her imagination and goes into character. She told Jack Hurst at the *Tennessean*, "When I'm writing I can be anywhere and anything that I want to be. If I'm writing about a dog or a cat—whatever I'm writing about, I am that thing. And I'm the kind of person that even the ugliest duckling is pretty to me, some way or another."

She approaches her writing by both scheduling time for creativity and making sure she is prepared at all times in case inspiration strikes. She says there is no particularly good place to come up with songs and ideas; they are constant and can happen anywhere, which is why she always carries a notebook, a pen, and a tape recorder with her when she's flying, traveling, or just walking around. She also keeps those tools next to her bed and bathtub or in the kitchen when she is cooking. She will wake up in the middle of the night to write down lyrics or a story for a song or a melody that she received in a dream. This way she never misses a note.

She can read only a little bit of music and writes everything down longhand—the words, chords, and notes to remember the melody. She says she can write anywhere, any time, for any reason. She usually writes with her guitar but also likes to work on the piano. Depending on what type of song she is working on or what kind of mood she wants to convey, she will experiment with the other instruments she plays—the banjo, the autoharp, and the dulcimer.

Like many successful and creative people, she has something of a process and schedule. When Andy Warhol talked to her for *Interview* magazine, he asked her what she had for breakfast and she told him that she usually has two breakfasts: coffee, toast, and jelly when she first wakes up well before the sun, and then, after her spiritual work and prayers, affirmations, and getting her business organized, she will have another. She does her best writing at 4:00 a.m., calling it "wee hour wisdom" and saying, "God's like a farmer. He gets up and throws out all of these ideas like corn, and I want to be the early bird."

It can take her anywhere from ten minutes to an hour to write a song, but she says some of her best songs take her about a half hour. And a lot of the time she can get something down on paper in a matter of minutes but then will go back and look it over and edit and revise until she gets it right.

Sometimes songs will come to her in the middle of a crowd or event and she will stop whatever she is doing and write it down on whatever is close to hand; if there is no paper around, she has been known to write it down on her hands. Over the years, Judy Ogle has been by her side to write things down for her if she gets inspired with an idea or a good line in the middle of something else. When she wrote "The Seeker," a heartfelt spiritual that she called a "talk with God," it came to her almost as a revelation and she said to Judy, "Write this down," and she dictated the song in about ten minutes. Dolly says it was one of the most profound religious experiences she ever had.

Her favorite way to write, however, is to find specific time away from the busyness of everyday life to go on retreat. She takes time off from touring or other work and hides out for a couple of weeks away from any and all distractions: "Don't bother me. Don't call me. I don't want to hear from nothing or nobody." She will go to one of her homes, fast for a few days in order to get spiritually anchored, and then pray and ask God for good ideas. Writing is a sacred exercise for her. "I have such definite thoughts, and that's kind of like my private time with God." Then she will "really kind of get in the spirit and really just let it flow and just write, write, write, write, write until I get tired of it and then I come back home." Finding the time for this type of writing binge is hard to come by but sounds pretty appealing, and effective.

But being creative isn't about zoning out and waiting for inspiration; it requires discipline, craft, and skill. And sometimes speed. When working on a project with someone else or for someone else, say a movie, a TV show, or a collaboration, you answer to many masters. When one is commissioned or assigned a creative project to do, things can get frustrating when everyone involved has an idea of what they want and you can keep revising and revising. When Dolly was writing the 9 to 5 musical, she found it difficult because she had so many different people telling her what to do and the script kept changing. Rolling with the punches and being flexible, not an ego-driven artiste, is a key part of being successfully creative. As they say, sometimes you have to kill your darlings. So don't be too precious about it.

One element of her writing is something she has never questioned, and that is her creative courage. She has always written what she feels at the moment, and her music spans different genres—old country, bluegrass, pop, gospel—and she isn't afraid to write about dark or unconventional subjects, like her earlier Southern gothic songs or taboo subjects from a female standpoint. "The Bargain Store" was banned by a lot of radio stations because people mistook the metaphor of being a used-up junk store as promoting prostitution, even though it was a song about heartbreak and trying to find a new love. In "Just Because I'm a Woman," she asked why it was okay for a husband or boyfriend to have previous lovers but not for the girlfriend or wife.

She says she never writes to be commercial and many of her songs are stories and don't follow the formula the Nashville establishment tried to teach her when she first started out. "They'd say, 'You have to have this, you have to have that, you've got to have two verses and a chorus.' But I never could get everything I wanted to say in two verses and a chorus. Some of the best songs I write just ramble on and on." She has a famous one-liner in which she says she had to get rich in order to write and sing like she was poor again. She also feels that her writing just gets better as she gets older, mostly because with age comes experience and, hopefully, wisdom. Despite the many mediums in which she has expressed her creativity, she considers herself a songwriter first and foremost, saying, "Songwriting is just as natural as breathing to me. Life's a song to me. That's how I express myself."

Coat of Many Colors

Dolly has been asked time and time again which of the songs she has written is her favorite. Sometimes she says it's "I Will Always Love You" but more often than not she says it is "Coat of Many Colors." "I have written thousands of songs, but that was more of an attitude, a philosophy, a way of life, and it addresses acceptance, bullying and the differences in people."

"Coat of Many Colors" came from a painful childhood story as well as the philosophy that her mother instilled in all of the Parton children. "We were poor, but she'd say, 'I don't want to hear that. We are not poor, just because we don't have money. We're rich in attitude, we're rich in spirit, we're rich in love.'"

Anyone who has listened to the lyrics—or seen the movie—knows the story. It was late fall and Dolly didn't have a coat to wear through the winter. A neighbor brought the family a box of rags, and Avie Lee sewed together a patchwork coat in time for Dolly to wear it for her first school picture when she was just nine. While she sewed, Avie Lee would tell the story from the Bible of Joseph and the special coat of many colors given to him by his father, which made his brothers so jealous. Dolly felt "so proud thinkin' I looked exactly like Joseph in my coat," but when she got to school, all the other kids made fun of her and in her school picture she managed to smile—for her mother's sake—through her tears.

Dolly has spoken about it at length: "That was a very sad and cutting memory that I long kept deep within myself. I remembered all the pain of it and the mockery. How the kids had tried to take my little coat off...and I didn't have a blouse on under it because I had done *well* just to have a little jacket to wear. So when the kids kept sayin' I didn't have a shirt on under it, I said I *did* because I was embarrassed. So they broke the buttons off my coat. They locked me in the coat closet that day and held the door closed and it was black dark in there and I just went into a screaming fit. I remembered all that and I was ashamed to even mention it and for *years* I held it in my mind."

When she got home, Avie Lee told Dolly, "I wouldn't worry about it. They're only looking with their eyes and you're looking with your heart." Dolly says that her mother's perspective changed hers and that since then that is how she tries to see things.

She turned that painful childhood experience into one of her most enduring songs. The story became the basis for the TV movie she produced and was nominated for an Emmy. She also made it into a children's book with a message about bullying. The song honored her mama, who loved it because it really made her look like a hero.

Be a Lifelong Learner

Dolly has always been a curious person and so much of her writing comes from paying attention to what is going on around her. If you aren't intellectually curious, you're never going to be a multidimensional, creative, or particularly interesting person. A dull or disengaged person is never going to write the all-American novel or songbook. Being committed to constantly growing and evolving as a person is crucial for creativity, as well as maintaining a zest for living.

Dolly's favorite movies: *Doctor Zhivago* and *Gone with the Wind*

Despite a general disinterest in school growing up, Dolly has a great love for learning and her intellectual curiosity is a big part of what makes her such a complex and compassionate person. She feels that even if you don't get a formal education, you can learn about and teach yourself everything through reading. She says that she reads fifty or more books a year.

Growing up, she says she read everything she could get her hands on: "The Bible, *The Farmer's Almanac*, *The Funeral Home Directory*, the directions and descriptions on the garden and flower seed packets, all medicine bottles, catalogs, and all kinds of mail, fairy tales, school books…" Now she likes to read the books on the *New York Times* bestseller list, as well as historical fiction and books about religion and philosophy. Rarely does a day go by when she doesn't pick up a book and read for a few minutes or a few hours, and feels that "a great book is like a new lover. You can't wait to get back to it." She says she is sometimes happiest sitting quietly at home reading a good book. Amen.

The Dolly Parton Library

- The Bible
- Agatha Christie mysteries
- *The Little Engine That Could* by Watty Piper: It makes perfect sense that this book is one of Dolly's favorites, with its main character's refrain of "I think I can, I think I can" as she struggles to get up the hill. It is one of the first books that Dolly remembers reading, and it is also the very first book every child who participates in the Imagination Library gets a copy of.
- Books on positive thinking and self-improvement: *The Power of Positive Thinking* by Norman Vincent Peale; *Possibility Thinking* by Robert H. Schuller; *The Magic of Believing* by Claude Bristol; *The Dynamic Laws of Prosperity* and *The Dynamic Laws of Healing* by Catherine Ponder; and *The Sleeping Prophet* by Edgar Cayce

- *New York Times* fiction bestsellers and historical fiction like *The Goldfinch* by Donna Tartt; *Orphan Train* by Christina Baker Kline; *The Fever Tree* by Jennifer McVeigh; *Peace Like a River* by Leif Enger; and *The Signature of All Things* by Elizabeth Gilbert.

Interestingly enough, outside of books and music, Dolly isn't much of an art lover. Her apartment with Sandy Gallin had an expansive art collection, including two Claes Oldenburgs and a Robert Rauschenberg. Dolly's said that a lot of the art was very expensive and she couldn't help but think, "Good Lord, I coulda done that in first grade!" She prefers the work of Ben Hampton, a Tennessee artist and naturalist whose rural scenes remind her of home. Gallin would tell her he was trying to cultivate an appreciation of high culture in her but she claims it didn't take. She once went to the opera in London with a friend and started snickering and giggling so much that she had to leave the theater. And once Sandy Gallin had Andy Warhol do a painting of her but neither one of them liked it—they thought she looked too harsh, almost masculine—and didn't buy it as a result. Just a few short years later, the painting was worth much more, about a million dollars more, than Sandy was going to pay for it, so he is the one who lost out.

Even if "culture" isn't your thing, nurturing your intellectual curiosity will keep you engaged and vibrant. Dolly believes in lifelong learning and doing your homework—not your school homework, but your life homework. Creativity is much broader than just being an artist. It's a way of solving problems, being innovative—all of which require thinking differently and having a well of experience to draw from. All creative pursuits stem from a desire for self-expression or an attempt to make sense of the human condition. You can't just sit around waiting for the muse to make a visit. You need to keep honing and expanding your skills and studying your craft, as well as keeping an open heart.

Not one to rest on her laurels, Dolly says she will never retire and will always stay curious. Asked about retirement, she says, "Why would I ever do that? That word doesn't register with me...I'm going to be productive, positive and work as long as I can." She keeps on working, exploring, and creating new things. She isn't afraid to expand her horizons. Living with that kind of passion and energy go hand in hand with being creative.

Dolly says it is better to wear out than rust out. This attitude goes beyond career advice; it is life advice. At age seventy, she put out a new album, *Pure & Simple*, an homage to her husband and marriage, and went on the biggest North American tour she had gone on in many, many years, traveling to sixty-three cities. Being on tour, with its rigorous schedule, living on the bus, and performing night after night, has put stars several decades younger than her in the hospital. Her enthusiasm and love for what she does never diminishes, and that seems to be the key to keeping on keeping on.

She says she wakes up with new dreams every day and feels like there is still so much for her to do. And the only way to really do that is to take care of yourself and be conscious of your habits and keep focusing your energy on the things you love. That advice works whether you are thirty, fifty, or seventy.

Dolly Songwriting Achievements

Dolly Parton is the most celebrated female country artist of all time. Her lifetime achievements could probably fill a book of its own. Her songwriting achievements are many:

- 32 Recording Industry Association of America–certified gold, platinum, and multiplatinum awards.
- 25 songs that have reached number one on the Billboard Country charts.
- 42 career top 10 country albums and 110 career charted singles over the past forty years. All-inclusive sales of singles, albums, hits collections, paid digital downloads, and compilation usage during her Hall of Fame career have reportedly topped a staggering 100 million records worldwide.
- 9 Grammy Awards, 12 Country Music Association Awards, 11 Academy of Country Music Awards, 3 American Music Awards. She is one of only five female artists to win the Country Music Association's Entertainer of the Year Award.

- Inducted as a member of the Country Music Hall of Fame in 1999.
- Winner of the CMA's Willie Nelson Lifetime Achievement Award.
- Kennedy Center Honors in 2006.
- 47 Grammy nominations and a Grammy Lifetime Achievement Award in 2011.
- 2 Oscar nominations—one for writing the title tune to *9 to 5* and the other for "Travelin' Thru" from the film *Transamerica.*

WWDD TO TAP INTO HER CREATIVITY?

- Find inspiration all around you and write down all of your ideas in a notebook.
- Be disciplined in devoting time to a creative life and come up with a process that works for you, whether waking up early or setting aside time for a creative "binge."
- The best way to stay engaged and vibrant in life is to nurture your intellectual curiosity.
- It's better to wear out than to rust out.
- Always be growing and learning.

Chapter Eleven

Charity Begins at Home

Philanthropy and Giving Back

*O*ver the years, Dolly has worked with charitable organizations in support of numerous causes, and her desire to give back is closely intertwined with her desire to help "my people"—her siblings and nieces and nephews and cousins and friends from back home as well as the rest of the people from the area where she grew up. She knows the disadvantages and struggles that they endure, having gone through them herself, and she wants to make life easier for them.

She told the *Tennessean* in 2015, "You want to feel like you're doing something good. I really feel proud as a citizen of this area, and just being a daughter of the hills here." Her philanthropic drive is intertwined with a deep pride in where she came from and a desire to help those from her poor region achieve their dreams the way she did hers. Dolly always said it "was a dream of mine to come back and do something great. And too, the Bible says, 'Honor your father and your mother,' and I wanted to bring honor to their name."

Giving back and helping others has more to do with her upbringing than with her religious background. She tells a story of meeting Colonel Sanders, the founder of Kentucky Fried Chicken, when she was a child. He looked her in the eye and told her, "You always pay your tithe." She does give away 10 percent of her gross income and says she gets it back a thousandfold. But she also distinguishes between tithing and charity. A tithe is giving a percentage of your income to a religious institution, or to acts of mercy or God. Charity is something that goes far beyond that to provide time or money or actions to help those who are less fortunate than you.

Part of that is just her big heart and part of it is having grown up in an environment where it was important to help your own. She knows that sharing your own dreams and success with others is a big part of a fulfilling life. The givin' is just as important as the gettin'.

"I love being able to do things that create opportunities for others, because that's when you learn that you've become more than just your success."

Give Where Your Heart Is

Dolly started small—from buying her family the first television in their hometown when she was just a child who earned money at Cas Walker's show, to buying band uniforms for her high school. She summed up her feelings about helping out her hometown pretty well when she made a public, heartfelt plea for aid to help the victims of the Smoky Mountain wildfires: "My family and my mountains are where my roots are and where my strength has always come from, especially during hard times. I've always thought of everyone in my family as My People. It's just the way we were raised—everybody is important and everybody takes care of each other. And it goes a lot farther than your kinfolk. Your neighbors are your family 'cause they take care of you, too, and I've always thought of everybody in my mountains as part of my family."

Dolly tends to give to causes that reflect the things that she didn't have growing up and that have an immediate impact on people's lives: education support, literacy programs, women's hospitals, and access to health care. All of these things were mostly absent in the hollers she grew up in, so she knows the importance of having them and how difficult it is to go without. Her mother went through twelve childbirths, half of them at home, because the Partons had neither the money nor the transportation to get to a hospital.

Back then, living out in the woods, they couldn't get to the doctor; the doctor came to them—when they were lucky. There wasn't really any other kind of medical care that didn't require a car and a lot of expense that was outside the reach of most people. Most of the time, when it came to medical care, they had to fend for themselves. Dolly tells the story of having three of the toes on her right foot almost cut off when she stepped on a broken mason jar and how her mother just sewed them back on with her regular darning needle with kerosene as anesthesia. The occasional bottle of castor oil was their way of fighting off illness.

To Dolly and her family and neighbors, Dr. Robert Thomas, who delivered Dolly, was a hero and his presence sometimes meant the difference between life and death. He made close to 1,000 house calls a year and traveled by horseback, by foot, or by jeep and would deliver babies, set broken bones, and provide vaccines. He eventually opened clinics to provide better medical care to the community. Dolly became the chairman of the Robert F. Thomas Foundation, in honor of Dr. Thomas, to help fund-raise and provide health care to her region. She gave $500,000 to open the Dolly Parton Wellness and Rehabilitation Center of Fort Sanders Regional Medical Center, which provides all of the women's health services that her mother never had. She also gave $1 million to Vanderbilt University Medical Center.

Many of the causes she supports have a specific place in her heart because of the people or creatures she has met and loved over the years. She has supported the Red Cross and

HIV/AIDS research, and she has helped animals and helped preserve her beloved Smoky Mountains. She earned the Partnership Award from the U.S. Fish and Wildlife Service in 2003 for her work in preserving the bald eagle through the American Eagle Foundation's sanctuary at Dollywood. There is a show there called *Wings of America* in which they educate the public about birds of prey. This show accepts donations that have helped rebuild the population of the American eagle and other birds in eastern Tennessee that were close to extinction.

Where Dolly gives her time and resources reflects the things that have specific meaning to her. No matter how big or small your giving, whether of time or money, focusing on the causes that are important to you and touch your heart will be the most meaningful and satisfying.

The Imagination Library

The dedication of her book *Dream More* reads, *This book is for my Daddy, who never learned to read and write, and paid a dear price for that, and inspired me to not let it happen to others.*

Dolly always loved her father and thought he was one of the smartest men she ever knew, but he couldn't write his own name or recognize his children's names if he saw them on a piece of paper. It broke her heart that his inability to read or write kept him so tightly bound to a cycle of never-ending backbreaking work. As mountain people, a lot of her own relatives and neighbors didn't go to school because they had to work from a young age to help feed the family. And those who did attend school didn't have a whole lot of reading material available to them, other than the Bible. As we know, Dolly used to read the old newspapers that were used as wallpaper in her home because there wasn't any other reading material around.

Dolly has said time and time again that one of the things she is the most proud of is starting the Imagination Library, which she launched in 1995 in her hometown of Sevier County to provide books as gifts to preschool children. Local parents can sign their child up and he or she will receive an age-appropriate book addressed just to them in the mail each month, starting with the day they are born and continuing until they reach age five. The program now provides more than 1 million books to young children a month (yes, 1 million books a *month*!) and has given away more than 100 million free books! For children! Pretty amazing.

Dolly says, "They call me the Book Lady. That's what the little kids say when they get their books in the mail," she told the *Washington Post* in 2006. "They think I bring them and put them in the mailbox myself, like Peter Rabbit or something."

The first book that was in the program was *The Little Engine That Could* because Dolly feels like she is the little engine that did. If you think you can, you can, and she wants that book to inspire in children everywhere a belief in themselves and perseverance, so they, too, can pursue their dreams, whatever they may be. Dolly says that "if you can read, you can find books on anything you want. You can self-educate even if you can't afford to go to school."

Her daddy was able to live long enough to see the impact of the Imagination Library and was prouder of her for that than for being a famous star. It made him feel like he had done something good too.

That's giving from your heart.

www.imaginationlibrary.com

Don't Provide a Handout, Provide a Hand Up

Despite disliking school and barely getting through high school, Dolly certainly understands the importance of education and feels it is the foundation for a better life. As far as she is concerned, you can never educate enough children. Knowing the hardships that children from her region deal with, she decided to provide some incentive to stay committed to school.

Dolly herself missed thirty-one days her first year of school. She also had a tough time dealing with not having the other things the better-off children had, and they made fun of her and her siblings for it. Beyond that, having to do family and household chores, keep up with homework, walk four miles to school—well, it is natural for her to want to help children who grew up as she did and motivate them to stay in school and get as much out of their education as they can. She was also bullied and there were terrible rumors spread about her in high school that made her want to drop out. But her mom told her to hold her head high and rise above it. She managed to graduate and was the first in her family to earn a diploma.

One of the first things Dolly did when she became successful in the 1970s was to start giving scholarships to kids who graduated at her old high school in Sevierville. Dolly created a buddy contract where students help each other stay in school. If they fulfill it, they get $1,000 to split between them upon graduation. Two students pledge to each other—and Dolly—that they won't drop out of school and will help each other out with any problems that might keep them from graduating. This can include problems with getting to and from school, having to work outside of school, bullying, teenage pregnancy, difficulties at home, emotional issues—you name it. There was one kid who got bullied at school because he had strong body odor, and as a result he kept getting into fights. It turned out he didn't have a mother or indoor plumbing, and he had no way to wash himself or his clothes properly. Through the buddy system, it was brought to the school's attention and they were able to give him a locker next to the showers so he could shower before or after school.

On a larger economic scale, when Dollywood opened in 1986 (which now includes the water park Splash Country and the dinner theaters Dolly Parton's Stampede and Smoky Mountain Adventures), Dolly hoped the business might bring work to the economically depressed Great Smoky Mountains region. It is now the largest employer in Sevier County. Dolly says she "knew Dollywood would be a great business for me, but I also knew it would generate a lot of money in that area and provide jobs. That's true success— when everybody's making money."

Dollywood is far more than a monument to a superstar; it honors the history and heritage of her people and has single-handedly lifted up the entire state of Tennessee. Dollywood sees more than 3 million visitors a year from all over the country and the world, and as a result, hotels, restaurants, entertainment, and many other businesses have been created. In fact, the area carries more of the state than Memphis or even Nashville! In a place where steady or year-round work can be extremely difficult to find, being able to employ 5,000 local people with your own company is a huge accomplishment. Being able to revive an entire region economically by creating an industry that feeds so many other businesses beyond your own—well, that's just power, pure and simple.

Granted, most people don't have that kind of power, but even the smallest entrepreneur or independent worker has the ability to contribute to the local economy and hire people—even if occasionally. The point is that instead of just donating money, looking at the bigger picture of helping people help themselves is what can have the most impact.

The Dolly Effect

In November 2016, a wildfire started in the Smoky Mountains and spread into the town of Gatlinburg, destroying homes and businesses and taking fourteen lives, including the wife and two children of one of Dollywood's employees. The devastation reached far and left many people with nothing—no home, no cars, belongings, or place to turn for help. The fires even spread as far as Dollywood and finally went out just at the edge of the beloved park that employs so many people in the area.

Dolly immediately rose to the occasion and within forty-eight hours started her My People Fund as part of the Dollywood Foundation to help the community. She made a heartfelt plea: "I hurt and grieved and prayed right along with them, and because I'm one of them and they are part of me, I knew that I had to do something to get my people through these hard times and see them land on their feet on the other side. That's what families do. That's what neighbors do . . . Part of why the people in the Smokies are my people is that when someone needs help, everybody steps up to do their part." It was clear where Dolly's work ethic came from, as well as those Smoky Mountain values of family, faith, and helping out your own.

She went on to ask everyone to help her and the Dollywood Foundation to raise money and received a tremendous response. Money was donated from individuals, businesses, and organizations from not only the United States but also all over the world. She also corralled other performers to raise millions for the Smoky Mountains Rise benefit telethon. She performed along with Reba McEntire, Kenny Rogers, and twenty other singers and friends of hers. Taylor Swift matched a $100,000 contribution from the Academy of Country Music for $200,000. Kenny Chesney and the Country Music Association each contributed $250,000, which helped kick off the fund-raising.

Dolly used her clout to raise awareness and money. If you are blessed enough to have that kind of influence, you have an obligation to use it.

All in all, $9 million was raised and went directly to the recovery efforts. Starting immediately, in December 2016, the My People Fund gave $1,000 a month to each of the 900 families whose homes were either destroyed or uninhabitable, whether they were homeowners or renters. They pledged to provide that for six months for a total of $6,000 per family so they could find shelter, food, and whatever else they needed. Anyone in need of help could go right to the Dollywood Foundation website and apply.

At six months, Dolly showed up to hand out the final

checks in person and to thank volunteers who helped in the effort. Because of the significant outpouring of donations, instead of giving that last check in the amount of $1,000, she gave each family $5,000, for a total of $10,000 per family.

Many of these details came from a bus driver and a cabdriver in the Pigeon Forge area, both of whom said they were incredibly proud of Dolly and what she has done for them. Unprompted, they shared the story of the wildfires and the employees from Dollywood who were so painfully affected. The bus driver said, "She has a heart of gold and never forgot where she came from. She came back here and helped us." Six months later the town of Gatlinburg was rebuilt and open for business. How did they do it? A lot of manpower and hard work. There was loss of life, loss of homes, and loss of livelihood, but the people just got up and got to work and didn't let it beat them down. Signs all over town proudly proclaimed "Mountain Strong!"

It is clear where Dolly gets her work ethic and strong desire to help others from. This isn't about providing more glory for herself. She sets a fine example of putting some of that compassion and effort into lifting up her friends, neighbors, and fellow human beings.

Charities and Foundations Supported by Dolly Parton

The causes Dolly is most dedicated to are those related to children, adoption, fostering and orphans, family and parent support, education, literacy, health, animals, cancer, diabetes, the creative arts, disaster relief, and veteran and military family support. Some of the organizations where she has dedicated her time and money are:

American Eagle Foundation
Barbara Davis Center for Childhood Diabetes
Boot Campaign
Cancer Research UK
Dogs Deserve Better
Dolly Parton Day Sevier High School Scholarships
Dollywood Foundation
Imagination Library
My People Fund
Operation Once in a Lifetime
The Red Cross
Robert F. Thomas Foundation
Save the Music Foundation

WWDD TO GIVE BACK?

- Give from your heart to the causes that are most important to you, starting at home.
- Donate your time, money, and efforts to providing things that will have an immediate impact on people's lives.
- Help people help themselves.
- If you have influence, rally and recruit those around you to help.
- Contributing to the local economy is also giving back and helping lift others up.
- Giving back isn't about glory for yourself; it's about lifting up your fellow human beings.

Think Through Your Legacy

*W*hile it pains us to think of a time when Dolly won't be with us, the fact is, we all leave this world at some point. What do you want to be remembered for? How do you want others to think of you or preserve your memory after you're gone? We only get one chance to go around in this life, so make it count. Leave the world a little—or a lot—better than it was when you came into it.

Dolly has spent a lot of time thinking about her legacy—personally, professionally, musically. She has shown this through the Dollywood Foundation and in creating things that will last long after she is gone. At the DreamMore Resort in Pigeon Forge, there is a carved wooden container in a glass case that is Dolly's "Dream Box." Made of chestnut with a small silver lock, it holds some of Dolly's memories and wishes for the future. The fact that it is made of chestnut is a tribute to her uncle and mentor, Bill Owens, who devoted a good part of his life working with the American Chestnut Foundation to develop and preserve a blight-resistant tree. It's not supposed to be opened until Dolly's one hundredth birthday, on January 19, 2046. What is inside is mostly a mystery, although there is one song, titled "My Place in History," that is to be released that day as her final song. What insights, hopes, and fulfilled dreams exist in those lyrics remain to be seen.

Her legacy goes far beyond the thousands of heartfelt songs she has written and performed. Dollywood, while full of "amusements" and exciting rides, is really a theme park that focuses on the history and heritage of her culture and is a testament to the love she has for her people from the Smoky Mountain area. It honors and celebrates the region's music, food, friendly people, and way of life. There is a large area devoted to local craftsmen and what, in some cases, are becoming lost arts: blacksmiths, candle makers, potters, glass blowers, woodworkers, and much more.

The Chasing Rainbows museum in Dollywood celebrates Dolly's life, including her humble beginnings to her work starting at age ten on Cas Walker's show; her hardships early on in Nashville; her big break on Porter Wagoner's show; her break into Hollywood, pop music, movies, and her countless television appearances and magazines; and her philanthropy and establishment of the Imagination Library. The museum is full of television clips, interviews, magazine covers, Grammy Awards, gold records, costumes and clothes, movie scripts—well, pretty much everything she has accomplished and done.

It is the ultimate tribute and one Dolly thought through carefully and designed with her fans and legacy in mind.

As Dolly said in her first memoir, she was hoping her ability to overcome her circumstances would be something that would not only inspire people, but also serve as an example that people could learn from. She wanted "to make life worth somethin' I can leave behind for somebody else to study and analyze when I'm gone."

She is a beloved legend in her own time, and indeed, beyond the course about her at the University of Tennessee, we can all study her, learn from her, and find our own inspiration to chase after our dreams. Her songs are her legacy, for sure, but her strong example of a life well lived, of making the most of what you've got, of living big, of her kindness and positive energy that lifts up the people around her, can inspire all of us. And assure us that we each leave our own, heartfelt, one-of-a-kind legacy.

Dolly, we will always love you!

Acknowledgments

My editor, Suzanne O'Neill, was enthusiastic and "got" this book from the very beginning. Her insightful and smart edits and advice hugely improved the manuscript—I couldn't have done this without her. Thank you to Nidhi Pugalia, who was helpful and engaged throughout this whole process and kept lines of communication open and everything organized. Thanks to the sharp marketing and publicity team at GCP— Jimmy Franco, Kamrun Nesa, and Tiffany Sanchez. Thanks to Carolyn Kurek for her smart copyedits, John Pelosi for his legal input, Claire Brown for guidance with illustrations and for designing such a fabulous cover, and Ben Sevier for being so supportive.

Steve Troha totally got this concept before I had written a word and made it possible for me to spend time away from my other work in order to do it. Thank you, Steve. Thank you also to Dado Derviskadic and Katherine Odom-Tomchin at Folio.

Monika Roe did a beautiful job of capturing the beauty,

energy, and essence of Dolly throughout her "eras" in the interior illustrations. And Libby van der Ploeg did a gorgeous job with the cover illustration.

Thank you to supportive friends, especially Ellie Rand, Marci Weisler, and Ann Wall, and to my family for being tolerant of my constant working and Dolly obsession, especially Liam, Maggie, Bill, and Paula.

Sources

Dolly's IMDB page shows 434 magazine and newspaper articles and interviews, and I have read through many of them. The following, however, were invaluable in pulling together her stories and overall philosophy of life:

Books

Berman, Connie. *The Official Dolly Parton Scrapbook*. Grossett and Dunlap, 1978.

Miller, Stephen. *Smart Blonde: Dolly Parton*. Omnibus Press, 2015.

Nash, Alanna. *Dolly*. Reed Books, 1978

Parton, Dolly. *Dolly: My Life and Other Unfinished Business*. New York: HarperCollins Publishers, 1994.

Parton, Dolly. *Dolly's Dixie Fixin's*. Viking Studio, 2006.

Parton, Dolly. *Dream More: Celebrate the Dreamer in You*. Riverhead Books, 2012.

Parton, Willadeene. *Smoky Mountain Memories: Stories from the Hearts of the Parton Family*. Rutledge Hill Press, 1996.

Schmidt, Randy L., ed. *Dolly on Dolly*. Chicago: Chicago Review Press, 2017.

Select Television Interviews/Videos

Barbara Walters, 1977 interview where Dolly spoke about her dreams for the future, most of which have since come true.

Oprah and Oprah.com.

The Today Show and Today.com

Assorted appearances on the Hallmark Channel.

Dolly's 2009 University of Tennessee Commencement speech.

Dave Grohl's "Nashville" episode on his *Sonic Highways* series on HBO. He interviews Dolly but also has amazing old footage of her as a child, as well as her first appearance singing "Dumb Blonde" on *The Porter Wagoner Show.*

Platinum Blonde, BBC documentary by Jenny Ash.

Select Movies

9 to 5

The Best Little Whorehouse in Texas

Steel Magnolias

Straight Talk

Joyful Noise

Coat of Many Colors, the fictional movie of her childhood, produced and narrated by Dolly

Christmas of Many Colors

Select Print Articles and Interviews

Chet Flippo's two *Rolling Stone* interviews from 1977 and December 11–19, 1980.

Lawrence Grobel's *Playboy* and *Playgirl* interviews.

Roger Ebert, 1980 and update.

Andy Warhol in *Interview* magazine.

TV Guide, November 27–December 3, 1993.

Amy Maclin, "I'll Have What She's Having," *O Magazine*, August 2017.

Meg Grant, piece in *AARP*, May/June 2009.

Several articles for *Southern Living* especially by Alanna Nash and Jennifer Cole.

Several articles in *Vogue*, especially one by MacKenzie Wagoner.

Interview with RuPaul in the 25th Anniversary issue of *Dazed*.

Several articles from the *New York Times*, especially by Bryan Miller, April 29, 1992.

Several articles in the *Guardian,* especially by Tom Lamont, December 2014.

There are several other key interviews and pieces that appeared in the following publications or websites: CNN, *Chicago Tribune*, *Washington Post*, Biography.com, *Elle* magazine, *People* magazine, *InStyle*, *Christian Today*, *Daily Mail*, the Boot, BBC, *Examiner, USA Today, First for Women*, the Huffington Post, *Tennessee Magazine, Knoxville News Sentinel, Tennessean*, LADYGUNN, Spotlight Country, Roughstock, *Mountaineer*, Sulphur-Springs News, *Telegram*, My Body and More, *Daily Tar Heel, Broken Records Magazine, Daily Herald* (Columbia), the A.V. Club, Grammy.com, AND MANY MORE.

Websites

Dollyparton.com

Imaginationlibrary.com

Dollywoodfoundation.com

Dollymania.net—T. Duane Gordon has been maintaining the definitive online Dolly Parton resource since 1998 and continues to update it regularly. His knowledge on all things Dolly is invaluable.

Dollywood

Thanks to all of the people at the Dollywood Dream-More Resort, Dolly Parton's Stampede, Dollywood, Splash

Country, and the Chasing Rainbows museum. The people I encountered in and around her hometown were some of the friendliest people I've ever met. They told some great firsthand stories about Dolly and what she has done for the region.

I'm also grateful to the people of Nashville, the Country Music Hall of Fame, and the Grand Ole Opry.

I'd also like to thank Maureen Crowe for her insight into the history of "I Will Always Love You"; Alex Michaels for his Dolly Parton makeup tutorial; and Rebecca Harrington for her humorous look at Dolly's diet in her book *I'll Have What She's Having.*

About the Author

Lisa Hancock

Lauren Marino is a writer, editor, and former publishing executive who has worked at Penguin, Random House, Hyperion, and HarperCollins publishers. She is the author of *Jackie and Cassini: A Fashion Love Affair.* She lives in New York City.